The
Quality
Manual

The entire contents of this book, including the text, diagrams and forms were created by the author using Aldus® Pagemaker.®

The
Quality
Manual

Terence J. Hall

The application of BS 5750
ISO 9001 EN 29001

JOHN WILEY
Chichester · New York · Brisbane · Toronto · Singapore

Copyright © 1992 by John Wiley & Sons Ltd,
Baffins Lane, Chichester,
West Sussex PO19 1UD, England

Reprinted September 1993

Other Wiley Editorial Offices

John Wiley & Sons, Inc., 605 Third Avenue,
New York, NY 10158-0012, USA

Jacaranda Wiley Ltd, G.P.O. Box 859, Brisbane,
Queensland 4001, Australia

John Wiley & Sons (Canada) Ltd, 22 Worcester Road,
Rexdale, Ontario M9W 1L1, Canada

John Wiley & Sons (SEA) Pte Ltd, 37 Jalan Pemimpin #05-04,
Block B, Union Industrial Building, Singapore 2057

Library of Congress Cataloging-in-Publication Data

Hall, Terence J.
    The quality manual : the application of BS 5750 / Terence J. Hall.
        p.   cm.
    Includes index.
    ISBN 0-471-93442-9 (pbk.)
    1. Quality control—Handbooks, manuals, etc.   I. Title.
    TS156.H27   1992   91–45797
                                                            CIP

British Library Cataloguing in Publication Data

A catalogue record for this book is
available from the British Library

ISBN 0-471-93442-9

Printed and bound in Great Britain by Redwood Books, Trowbridge, Wiltshire.

Contents

Continued overleaf

Contents

Part 3

Quality Assurance

Introduction

INTRODUCTION TO THIS BOOK

This book has been produced principally as a guide to the installation of BS 5750 within a company, although I can visualise the situation where the reader may be simply seeking to improve or expand a Quality System already in place. It may well be that you are not seeking BS 5750 registration at this time but would like to install a system for the sake of internal efficiency or perhaps as a trial. Whatever your reasons, the design of the book is intentionally arranged so that it could in itself be used as the foundation for your own company's Quality Management System.

Part 2 of this book (blue pages) is a basic Quality Manual which the reader may wish to adapt for company use. This could be achieved a number of ways; it could be simply abstracted en bloc, or retyped around your own ideas. One option open to you is to fill in the software application form at the back of the book. This will bring you the "softcopy" version of the material and the set of forms in Part 3 of this manual.

It was decided not to include the "softcopy" versions of the material with this book for a number of sound reasons. Firstly we may update the text and anyone sending in for a copy will hopefully receive an enhanced version. Within the covers of a book is not the most secure place to hold magnetic media - by the time you get round to needing them them they may have gone missing. There is also the question these days of format, disk size and density. Finally, this book may find itself in environments hostile to the safe keeping of magnetic media, with the result that when you get down to needing the disks they are unreadable.

This book has been modelled around BS 5750 Part 1, since Part 1 has clauses to cover the areas of Design, Development, Production, Installation and Service - whereas BS 5750 Part 2 only covers the Production and Installation elements; so we conveniently embrace everything by studying Part 1 (see Table on next page). There is a BS 5750 Part 3 which deals exclusively with the final inspection and testing of a product, but this application of the Standard is less common and so I am excluding it.

The introduction of a Quality System is not as many people seem to think, simply a case of documenting what you are currently doing. It should start with a total re-examination of your current practices and processes. Take the opportunity to get 'dead wood' out of the system and improve what is left

BS 5750 Part	**ISO**	**APPLICATION**
0 (1987) Section 0.1	9000	**GUIDE** to the selection and use of the Standard.
0 (1987) Section 0.2	9004	**GUIDE** to quality management and quality system elements.
1 (1987)	9001	**SPECIFICATION** for design/development, production, installation and servicing.
2 (1987)	9002	**SPECIFICATION** for production and installation.
3 (1987)	9003	**SPECIFICATION** for final inspection and testing.
4 (1981)	none	**GUIDE** to the use of BS 5750 Part 1.
5 (1981)	none	**GUIDE** to the use of BS 5750 Part 2.
6 (1981)	none	**GUIDE** to the use of BS 5750 Part 3.

Other related Standards:

BS 4778 (1987)	**GLOSSARY** of terms used in quality assurance (including reliability and maintainability).
BS 4891	**GUIDE** to quality assurance.
BS 5701	**GUIDE** to number defective charts for quality control.
BS 5702	Quality control charts for variables (revision of BS 2564).
BS 5703	**GUIDE** to data analysis & quality control by cusum techniques.
BS 5781	Part 1 - Measurement and calibration systems. Part 2 - **GUIDE** to Part 1 of BS 5781.
BS 6143	**GUIDE** to the determination and use of quality related costs.

while introducing any new procedure which your investigation suggests would be beneficial. Then build into the process a range of checks, audits and reviews to ensure the process continues to operate as it was designed to. Avoid the temptation to include in your Quality System areas of the business which have no bearing on the Quality of your product or service. Too frequently I see topics like fire drill, holiday rotas, office cleaning included in the scheme. Such things may well be important, but they have nothing to do with BS 5750 and simply clutter up the concept.

There are, no doubt, many sound reasons for introducing your company to a Quality Management System, but let me focus on just a few of perhaps the key justifications as I see them.

MARKETPLACE

More and more business organisations are requiring BS 5750 as a condition of tender for any contract made with them. The signs are that this is increasing. So if you don't take this path you are going to lose business opportunities.

COST-EFFICIENCY

There may be an initial call on resources and undoubtedly some "set-up" costs involved to put a Quality System in place. However, once the initial investment has been made a Quality System is a net saving exercise. It will reduce waste, which means it will remove unnecessary expense; it will reduce unnecessary activity and therefore increase efficiency.

MORALE

People like to be associated with Quality and to work in an efficient, well run company. They also like to be active contributors and be recognised for their efforts towards the improvements. A Quality System allows you to quickly discover those people who are good performers and reward them. It also allows you to recognise those in need of help and instruction.

CUSTOMER SATISFACTION

It is an undeniable fact that if your company is supplying Quality goods and service from an efficient organisation staffed with well motivated employees, then you will not be able to keep it a secret from your customers for very long.

NEW ERA plc - A SAMPLE COMPANY

It is difficult to generate a Quality System totally in abstract terms. It is far better understood if one can relate it to a real organisation or at least a realistic model. The company described in this book, "New Era plc", is an imaginary one, created not to make a fortune for its shareholders but to provide a vehicle to illustrate the application of BS 5750. I hope my readers will forgive me if my imagination has produced a company that fails to reflect their own, but I beg even further indulgence if by chance it appears to be a carbon copy. The organisation chart shown below gives you an overview of the structure of the "New Era" company. Those departments and posts shown in shaded boxes, although making an important and useful contribution to the corporate venture, have only limited and peripheral involvement with the BS 5750 Registration or Quality System of New Era plc.

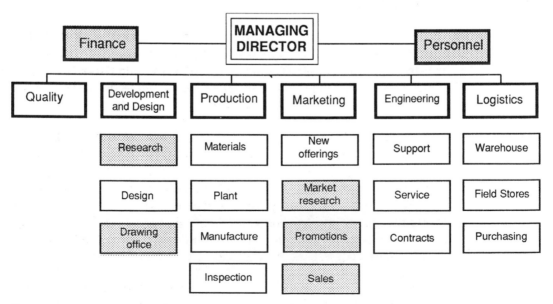

Structure of New Era plc

LAYOUT AND PAGE NUMBERING

THE LAYOUT OF THIS BOOK

This manual has been organised into four major parts. I have tried to build into it an easy-to-use numbering method with an architectural logic to help find your way around the contents. You will also see that the numbering scheme used in Parts 1 and 2 directly cross relates to the clauses of BS 5750 Part 1 (1987).

For example, BS 5750 - Part 1, *Clause 4.5* relates to "Documentation" and you will find that my Part 1, *Topic 4.5* discusses the same subject. This logic then follows through into Part 2, where *Section 4.5* also deals with documentation. This pattern has been maintained throughout the book wherever practical.

PAGE NUMBERING

I am sure my reader is accustomed to finding a book starting with Page 1 followed by Page 2 and continuing this simple sequence until they reach the back cover. The numbers at the foot of each page in this book follow this convention. For ease of use the index at the end of the book fits this numbering scheme.

However, in Quality documentation, where it is often necessary to add and delete pages, such a method of numbering pages can be a handicap. For this reason I have provided an alternative scheme across the top of the page, giving each its own unique identity and the page numbers within this scheme only extend to the end of that particular subject.

Parts 0, 1 and 2 of this book have been presented in this way (across the top of the page) so as to provide you with a working example of how you should construct the documentation within your own Quality System. Page numbering could be expressed in a variety of perfectly acceptable ways. You will frequently see, in Quality System documentation, the *Page 1 of 2* followed by *Page 2 of 2* method used . The limitation of that format is that when you need to extend the text for a Procedure or Work Instruction at the end of a section you have to adjust the numbering on every page and therefore need to reissue the whole set. I have adopted a method which is both neat and more flexible. The last page number within a group of pages has a *minus* sign behind it, while all the rest have a *plus.* I think the advantages of this method are obvious.

QUALITY ASSURANCE AND ITS HISTORY

QUALITY ASSURANCE - WHAT IS IT ?

I really have to start this book by defining terms. I do hear a lot of nonsense these days about Quality and almost every advertisement hoarding appears to claim some company or another to be associated with this desirable attribute. So what is a Quality Product or Service? Since my reader can't enter into a debate on the matter, I would like to simply offer you an apt definition which I came across some years ago. I've yet to see a better definition and until I do I'll stick with this:

Quality = in conformance with user requirements

If you want to take out the fancy words and substitute them with more or less everyday words, then you can render it down to:

Quality = **Fitness for use**

To illustrate this point could I suggest that no matter how highly you might regard the Rolls Royce "Chamade" - if you are a farmer wanting to get around a 500-acre estate then the Land Rover is the *quality* vehicle.

A BRIEF HISTORY

The history of British Standards can be traced back to the turn of the century when there was a desperate need in Britain to rationalise the variations in rolled steel girders being made. At that time there were no fewer than 75 different versions of tramway rails! When the steel rolling industry established a standard for rails the choice was reduced down to just five.

It wasn't until the lessons of World Way 2 had been learned that the value of Quality Assurance began to emerge, first in the USA, where the original concepts were formulated, and later in Europe through NATO in what became the AQAP (Allied Quality Assurance Publication) series of documents. These gave guidelines on such matters as production efficiency, selection of suppliers and many of the key aims now embodied in today's International Standards.

9

The American AQAP series were eventually adopted in the UK by the Ministry of Defence as guidance on procurement for the British Armed Forces; these were known as "DEF STANS". The value of these standards was not lost on British industry where, in the 1960s, many of the larger organisations began to develop their own versions of Quality Control and Quality Assurance(QA).

It was no surprise to find that these organisations began to pass down the conditions of QA imposed on them to their own suppliers, and, like the "flea on the back of the dog", so it went on. This approach may well have been influential in making suppliers look more carefully at their output and methods of working and to changing their attitude towards QA. But it was the diversity of requirements set out by all these different organisations which in itself was now producing the problem, and some rationalisation into a common base was desperately needed.

When BS 5750 was introduced in 1979 it was seen as the solution. Here was a quite different approach to Quality Assurance, where the focus was to do things right in the first place rather than the retrospective, and more expensive, doctrine of inspection for faults after the event. BS 5750 was so effective that it was adopted almost as it stood by the International Standardisation Organisation when it published its ISO 9000 in 1987. At the same time the European Standard EN 29000 was launched, exactly mirroring the BS and ISO papers.

QUALITY IMPROVEMENTS

WHERE TO START ?

In a year's time you are going to be asking yourself "How do I know what effect all this activity has had on the performance of my team, and on the perception of the service we provide, as seen by the customers?" Well unless you take a reading of the situation as it is today, you will never be able to make a truly objective measurement. It follows, therefore, that the very first Quality Project you should assign to someone (or do it yourself) is carry out a couple of surveys, one targeting all, or a representative set, of the customers and the other taking a sample measure of the morale of the team.

CUSTOMER PERCEPTION OF SERVICE

Forgive me if I use Field Service Engineering as a case study but it is an area I know well and it is very similar to many "deliverable" services. Your own company may well carry out some form of Customer Satisfaction Survey already and it may be possible to extract from that a group of relevant questions, along with the results, which relate to Field Engineering. If this is the case then half the work has been done for you. If not, you need to create a short survey form targeted around questions like:

- How do you rate being able to place a request for service ?
- How effective are our engineers in fixing the problem?
- Do they appear to be professional?
- How good are they at listening to what you have to say?
- Do they seem to carry the spare parts they need?
- Is the equipment returned to you cleaned?
- How would you assess the people in the office (i.e. on the phone)?

I'm sure you can develop a short set of questions which would best suit your particular type of activity and customer base. The aim is to establish a "reference level" that can record where you stand today with the customers. It should also show you where your effort ought to be placed to get the optimum improvement. Finally, it will enable you to see, in a year's time, how effective you have been when you carry out the survey again. A final plea - don't change the questions between the two surveys. It sounds a foolish thing to mention but you might be surprised at the number of companies who do just that!

Can I suggest that, since you are asking the customers to use their valuable time filling in your form, you might think about offering them some form of incentive, like an entry into a draw for a small prize. It would also be polite to post back to them the accumulated results.

From the survey results you should, in consultation with your staff, be able to pin-point a number of customer concerns that could be effectively addressed by means of Quality Improvement Projects (see Quality Circles).

CONSTANT ROLLING VIEW APPROACH

An alternative approach to the task of measuring customer satisfaction in a "on-site service delivery" environment is to make every service visit an opportunity to collect the customer's perception of your company's response to their needs. Since the customer may have to sign some sort of form at the end of a visit, it is not difficult to get him to tick a few boxes on the same piece of paper to express a few views on the service he has just received (see Form E1902 in Part 3).

MORALE OF YOUR PEOPLE

Now let us turn to the question of the morale of your people. If that's low, then your efforts towards improving customer satisfaction is going to be met with some resistance. A demoralised workforce is just what you don't need while you are attempting to put a Quality System in place and improve the service to your customers. Let us believe they are not actually demoralised but I would like to bet there are sceptics among them who are not convinced by it all. And if there are, well, you had better know now, so you can do something constructive about it.

Most companies these days run some form of annual Employee Satisfaction Survey; many use outside agencies to conduct them. These surveys tend to look at the employee from a corporate perception. They want the "big" picture on the "big" issues. What you need to know about is the local issues, the equity of individual workloads, the support available to your people when they are are up against a difficult technical problem, the acceptability of the current shift/overtime arrangements and so on. You will notice I am listing things which could be sorted out locally, not issues which will need a change of attitude by the Board of Directors.

You need to know how your people feel about the service they are providing to the customers and towards the infrastructure you have in place to help them. In exactly the same way as was suggested for the Customer Satisfaction Survey, you need at least a "snap-shot" of their opinion as it stands today so that you will be able to gauge what progress you have made in a year's time.

This quest to discover what improvements are needed links up very nicely with the purpose of the Quality Circles which are described in Topic 5 of this part of the book. Once you have carried out a survey you should be able to target the Quality Circles right into the areas which will provide the maximum reward.

MORALE INDEX

Within a survey it is frequently the practice to have five or six questions which never change from one year to the next. It is these which you can use to arrive at an arithmetic mean and use that as a Morale Index. They are usually questions which relate directly to the staff and their ability to carry out their duties and would perhaps cover areas such as:

- The nature of the work they are called upon to carry out.
- The support they get from the rest of the department.
- The training, both technical and non-technical, they receive.

The idea is that over a number of surveys (as long as you keep this set of key questions locked into it) you have a foundation parameter you can use to monitor the shifting sands of employee satisfaction.

FEEDBACK

Don't forget that you owe a prompt feedback to the people who took the trouble to answer your opinion survey, in the form of at least a summary of the results. I personally would go a step further and let them know how I interpret the findings. I might also provide them with at least one or two actions that I intend to take as a direct result of their expressed opinion.

You will discover that memories are short when it comes to opinion surveys. To make sure people realise that their views were listened to and acted on you should make it clear, whenever you put an improvement in place, that it is a consequence of an adverse opinion they had expressed at the time of the survey.

REGISTRATION

OBTAINING REGISTRATION TO BS 5750

You may decide that the lack of Quality Assurance experience in your organisation prompts you to seek "outside help", particularly in the early stages of setting it up. There are many reliable, independent consultants who will, for a fee, guide you through the metamorphosis of installing BS 5750. They can be good value since their presence will get you over the initial intensive effort to adapt the Standard into the working practices of your company. They will have the experience of the required documentation and just setting that up can be a large "one time" up-front investment of time.

There are currently 18 accreditation bodies in the UK who can examine a company seeking registration to BS 5750. Some of these specialise in specific sectors of industry, such as The Quality Scheme for Ready Mixed Concrete. Accreditation starts by you sending in copies of your documentation so that the selected accreditation body can make its evaluation and see how you have said the processes are intended to function within your company. They may also give you the opportunity to make whatever changes they would like to see in the Quality Manual or Procedures. A date will be agreed for the assessment and they will generally give you an estimate of the costs because they will at this stage, having seen your documentation, have a better idea of how many man-hours will be needed to conduct the assessment.

ASSESSMENT DAY

On the agreed date the team of inspectors from the accreditation body will arrive with a plan of the areas they intend to audit already in their briefcases, and they will have drawn up a schedule of who and what they wish to see. You need to make a number of arrangements in advance.

First impressions count; it is rather nice to arrive at a company to find not only that you were expected but that a car parking space had been reserved for you, and a visitors badge all made out ready. A room will be needed where an opening meeting can take place. This meeting is to both allow all the parties to get to know each other and for the visiting inspectors to describe their intended plan. It is usual at this meeting for a senior manager from the company to greet the visitors and give a *brief* description of the company. This same room (or a similar sized room), should be set aside for the inspectors to use as an office for the duration of their stay.

You need to appoint a member of your own staff as host/guide to each of the inspectors on the team.

It goes without saying that these inspectors need to eat just like the rest of us but don't waste your time and theirs with formal lengthy breaks. They will want to get on with the work they came to do. I was once taken out to lunch in the middle of an assessment to a restaurant which seemed to specialise in making lunch last two hours! It became evident what the company I was assessing were doing; they thought that the less time I spent on the actual inspection the better. It back-fired; I extended the audit half a day to find out just what it was they didn't want me to see.

Having been through this exercise from both sides of the fence as it were; my advice is to be open with them on the things *they ask* about. But at the same time *don't volunteer* information they never requested; it may lead them down a path you wished they hadn't trodden. They're not fools; they have had a lot of experience of both BS 5750 and your industry and can quickly detect waffle and prevarication.

If there is time the inspectors may agree to give you a short informal feedback at the end of each day. This may give you the chance to put right a few of the discrepancies as the assessment proceeds, but don't bank on it, there may not be enough time. The important meeting is at the end of their inspection, once they have had enough time to complete their report. The final half day is usually taken up with the writing of their report and their private deliberations on what each member of the inspection team thought of your company against the terms of the Standard. Once the report is ready the company representatives are invited back into the meeting so they can be told of the conclusion. They normally will give you a detailed feedback on what they saw, what was good and what needs additional attention. You will be provided with this written report there on the day and part of that report will be any noncompliances that they uncovered in the course of their inspection. Noncompliances or discrepancies are not always an indication that you have failed but are something you will have to put right within an agreed timetable.

When the number of noncompliances are either abnormally high or, if not numerous, then of a serious nature, you will be failed. But hopefully, because you have read this book, you will *pass*. Even then when you pass, there are always some noncompliances left for you to resolve and you will be required to write in by an agreed date that you have either corrected the problems or provide them with a reasonable and acceptable target date when

16

resolutions will be in place. My advice to you, following your initial assessment, would be to re-investigate each noncompliance or discrepancy raised for yourself following up a reported resolution by someone in your company. My reason for saying this is twofold; firstly, you will need to have reliable evidence of the corrective action taken, and secondly you will then be able to confirm that the correction of this problem has not simply created another.

There is one other variation I have come across which I should mention, and that is being given a Provisional Pass on condition that certain things are put right quickly. The accreditation body will want to see positive evidence of the correction before you will be issued with a certificate. They may even require to return to site and check for themselves that the problem has been fixed. This is a preferable option to actually being failed and having to go to the back of the queue and start again.

QUALITY ASSESSMENT SCHEDULES

One is able to apply BS 5750 to many diverse sectors of business activity, ranging from the manufacturing of building bricks to the repair of refrigerators, with quite surprising alignment. However, there are unique features to every commercial endeavour and for this reason BS 5750 frequently requires some additional "focus", as it were. This is where Quality Assessment Schedules (QASs) come into the story. I should point out that the name QAS is what the British Standards Institution (BSI) call their Schedules. Other titles for these schedules are to be found in use by the other accreditation bodies but for simplicity I will refer in this section exclusively to the BSI series of QASs.

One of the key strengths of the QAS scheme is that the relevant authorities in a specific sector of industry or business get to make a contribution as to the scope and application of the QAS designed for their industry sector. If we take one such example, then perhaps QAS/3460/361, which applies to the maintenance of domestic electrical 'white goods' is fairly typical. This QAS was drawn up by BSI with the participation of the Electricity Boards around at the time (this was pre-privatisation) and The Association of Manufacturers of Domestic Electrical Appliances. Various other organisations were consulted to add the viewpoint of the customers. If one looks at the outcome of these deliberations and what the QAS eventually embraces one begins to see their value.

In the case of QAS/3460/361 it sets out such things as:

- In the case of a home repair service, then "within 3 working days" is to be offered.
- That 80% of all repairs should be fixed on the engineer's first visit.
- The engineer may service a unit he has not been trained on providing the customer understands that this is the situation.
- Both the repair and the parts used are to carry a minimum 12 months guarantee.
- At the completion of the work the customer is to be provided with a "Statement of Completed Work".

I know of over 50 of these *sector schemes* currently in use and generally every registration to BS 5750 by an organisation also includes at least one of these specialised specifications as an extension to the scope of the BS 5750 registration. You will find a two page listing of quite a number of QASs in Appendix A at the end of this Topic.

STANDARD INDUSTRIAL CLASSIFICATION (SIC)

SIC codes, as they are known, are referred to as *individual schemes* and give a company the opportunity to have the BS 5750 registration more exactly tailored to its particular area of business. This is especially useful when the activity of the company seeking registration doesn't readily align with any of the established "sector schemes". If I quote a few examples you will see my point - wines and cider, printing and publishing and cleaning services. You might, for example, these days come across a company registered to the BS 5750 and SIC 9811 and this second identifier tells you which individual scheme is applicable;   SIC 9811 happens to be for laundries. There are numerous categories of SIC codes, enabling almost any sector of business to be precisely targeted, and I think there is a move towards these codes eventually replacing the QAS.

SURVEILLANCE

Once you have the registration you are able to announce the fact to the world and begin to see some return for all the work you did setting things in place. But that's not the end of the story by any means; you have to maintain the momentum and keep it all working. To an agreed schedule the accreditation body will send a representative back to your company, sometimes with very little preannouncement, to carry out surveillances. They will expect to find evidence that what you said at the time of the original assessment is genuinely taking place. Here again, you can expect to be presented with noncompliances if the inspector discovers that your practices are not following the stated intent.

Don't regard noncompliances that the inspectors uncover in totally negative terms. They expect to find a few items not quite as they should be; after all, they look at your company with a independent and perhaps fresh viewpoint. These inspectors are not allowed to tell you how to fix things - how you run your company is your business - but you would be well advised to listen carefully to them since you can pick up some very good ideas. One last point regarding surveillance visits by the accreditation body (e.g. BSI); be most careful not to allow them to be a subsitute for your own Quality Auditing Programme (see Part 1 Topic 4.17). The Standard states quite clearly that you must have a comprehensive system of your own in place.

ACCREDITATION BODIES

	Key

Associated Offices Quality Certification Ltd — Key 1
Longridge House, Longridge Place, Manchester M60 4DT.
(061-833-2295)

ASTA Certification Services — Key 1
23-24 Market Place, Rugby CV21 3DU.
(0788-578435)

BSI Quality Assurance — Key 1 & 2
PO Box 375, Linford Wood, Milton Keynes, MK14 6LL.
(0908-220908)

British Approvals Services for Electric Cables — Key 1
Silbury Boulevard, Milton Keynes MK9 2AF.
(0908-691121)

Bureau Veritas Quality International Ltd — Key 1
70 Borough High Street, London SE1 1XF.
(071-378-8113)

Central Certification Services Ltd — Key 1
Victoria House, 123 Midland Road, Wellingborough,
Northants NN8 1LU.
(0933-441796)

Ceramic Industry Certification Scheme Ltd — Key 1 & 2
Queens Road, Penkhull, Stoke on Trent ST4 7LQ.
(0782-411008)

Construction Quality Assurance — Key 1
Arcade Chambers, The Arcade, Market Place,
Newark, Notts NG24 1UD.
(0636-708700)

Det Norske Veritas Quality Assurance Ltd — Key 1
Veritas House, 112 Station Road, Sidcup, Kent DA15 7BU.
(081-309-7477)

Engineering Inspection Authorities Board — Key 1
c/o Institute of Mechanical Engineers.
1 Birdcage Walk, London SW1H 9JJ.
(071-973-1271)

Key

Lloyd's Register Quality Assurance Ltd   1
Norfolk House, Wellesley Road, Croydon CR9 2DT.
(081-688-6883)

The Loss Prevention Certification Board Ltd   1 & 2
Melrose Avenue, Boreham Wood, Herts WD6 2BJ.
(081-207-2345)

National Inspection Council Quality Assurance Ltd   1
5 Cotswold Business Park, Millfield Lane, Caddington,
Beds LU1 4AR.
(0582-841144)

The Quality Scheme for Ready Mixed Concrete   2
3 High Street, Hampton, Middx TW122SQ.
(081-941 0273)

Sira Certification Service   1 & 2
Saighton Lane, Saighton, Chester CH3 6EG.
(0244-332200)

TRADA QAS Ltd   1
Stocking Lane, Hughenden Valley, High Wycombe,
Bucks HP14 4NR.
(0240-245484)

UK Certification Authority for Reinforcing Steels   1 & 2
Oak House, Tubs Hill, Sevenoaks, Kent TN13 1BL.
(0732-450000)

Yarsley Quality Assured Firms Ltd   1
Trowers Way, Redhill, Surrey RH1 2JN.
(0737-768445)

Source of list:

National Accreditation Council for Certification Bodies
19 Buckingham Gate, London SW1E 6LB.
(071-233-7111)

Key: 1 = Quality Management Systems to BS 5750.
       2 = Product Conformity Certification.

Listing of Quality Assessment Schedules to BS 5750 (REGISTERED FIRM - sector scheme)

QAS 2210/142	MANUFACTURE OF STEEL INGOTS AND WROUGHT PRODUCTS
QAS 2234/74	MANUFACTURE OF MILD STEEL WIRE
QAS 2418/48	CLAY BRICKS AND SPECIAL SHAPES
QAS 2437/49	PRECAST CONCRETE MASONRY UNITS
QAS 2481/109	MANUFACTURE OF REFRACTORY PRODUCTS
QAS 2514/178	MANUFACTURE OF PLASTIC MATERIALS WITHOUT LOT TRACEABILITY
QAS 2514/282	MANUFACTURE AND SUPPLY OF RESINS AND ANCILLARY PRODUCTS
QAS 2551/201	MANUFACTURE OF PAINT PRODUCTS
QAS 2567/349	THE PRODUCT DEVELOPMENT, PRODUCTION & SUPPLY OF SEALANTS, ADHESIVES & BUILDING CHEMICALS.
QAS 2567/350	PRODUCTION AND SUPPLY OF SEALANTS, ADHESIVES & BUILDING CHEMICALS
QAS 3111/113	IRON CASTINGS
QAS 3120/10	TOE CAPS FOR SAFETY FOOTWEAR
QAS 3120/143	MANUFACTURE OF FERROUS AND NON-FERROUS FORGINGS
QAS 3138/187	HEAT TREATMENT OF METALS
QAS 3138/20	METAL FINISHING, INCLUDING SURFACE TREATMENT
QAS 3138/294	HOT DIP GALVANIZING OF PRODUCTS AFTER MANUFACTURE
QAS 3163/351	MANUFACTURE OF DOMESTIC HOT WATER STORAGE AND BUILT-UNDER DOMESTIC GAS COOKING APPLIANCES
QAS 3169.4	MISCELLANEOUS FINISHED METAL PRODUCTS NOT ELSEWHERE SPECIFIED
QAS 3169.4/9	PORTABLE FIRE EXTINGUISHERS
QAS 3221/277	DESIGN, MANUFACTURE & INSTALLATION OF MACHINE TOOLS AND MACHINE TOOL EQUIPMENT
QAS 3284/150	HEATING, VENTILATING & AIR CONDITIONING EQUIPMENT & COMPONENTS
QAS 3289/16	MACHINING AND METAL-FORMING PROCESSES WITH LOT TRACEABILITY
QAS 3289/17	MACHINING AND METAL-FORMING PROCESSES WITHOUT LOT TRACEABILITY
QAS 3289/31	STEEL FABRICATIONS REQUIRING LOT TRACEABILITY
QAS 3289/32	STEEL FABRICATIONS
QAS 3289/87	DESIGN AND MANUFACTURE OF MECHANICAL ASSEMBLIES
QAS 3301/302	MANUFACTURE AND INSTALLATION OF EQUIPMENT TO MEET IEC 950
QAS 3301/317	THE REPAIR AND MAINTENANCE OF ELECTRICAL/ELECTRONIC EQUIPMENT INSTALLED IN OFFICES
QAS 3302/187	MAINTENANCE SERVICES FOR ELECTRONIC COMPUTER EQUIPMENT
QAS 3302/355	CUSTOMER SOFTWARE ENGINEERING SUPPORT AND MAINTENANCE SERVICES FOR COMPUTER SOFTWARE SYSTEMS
QAS 3302/79	DESIGN, REPLICATION & DISTRIBUTION OF APPLICATION SOFTWARE FOR USE IN ECSE
QAG 3302/40	DESIGN, DEVELOPMENT, PRODUCTION AND INSTALLATION OF COMPUTER SYSTEM EQUIPMENT
QAG 3302/356	COMPUTER-BASED INFORMATION SERVICES SUPPLIED BY BUREAUX (INTERNAL OR EXTERNAL)
QAG 3320/190	DESIGN, MANUFACTURE AND INSTALLATION OF "TURNKEY" SYSTEMS
QAS 34 /51	MANUFACTURE AND INSTALLATION OF ELECTRICAL/ELECTRONIC DEVICES
QAS 34 /60	REPAIR OF SPECIALIST ELECTRICAL EQUIPMENT
QAS 34 /61	DESIGN, MANUFACTURE AND INSTALLATION OF ELECTRICAL/ELECTRONIC DEVICES, ASSEMBLES & UNITS

QAS 3433/173	MANUFACTURE & INSTALLATION OF ELECTRO-MECHANICAL INTRUDER ALARMS
QAS 3442/162	ELECTRONIC EQUIPMENT AND SYSTEMS MAINTAINERS
QAS 3442/354	SALE, REPAIR & MAINTENANCE OF ELECTRICAL & MECHANICAL EQUIPMENT FOR THE ELECTRICAL MACHINERY TRADES
QAS 3443/327	INSTALLATION, COMMISSIONING AND TEST OF CIVIL LAND MOBILE RADIO EQUIPMENT IN VEHICLES
QAS 3443/328	INSTALLATION, COMMISSIONING AND TEST OF CIVIL LAND MOBILE RADIO EQUIPMENT IN FIXED STATIONS
QAS 3443/329	FIELD MAINTAINERS AND REPAIRERS OF CIVIL LAND MOBILE RADIO EQUIPMENT
QAS 3444/56	CABLE ASSEMBLIES AND WIRING HARNESSES
QAS 3460/361	SERVICING OF MAJOR DOMESTIC ELECTRICAL APPLIANCES AND DOMESTIC ELECTRICAL INSTALLATIONS
QAS 3640/65	MATERIALS FOR AEROSPACE
QAS 453/95	MANUFACTURE OF CLOTHING AND KNITTED GARMENTS
QAS 4630/5	SUPPLY AND ERECTION OF FENCES
QAS 4725/128	MANUFACTURE OF FLUTED CARDBOARD CARTONS
QAS 4836/22	MOULDED & EXTRUDED PLASTIC PRODUCTS AND COMPONENTS WITH LOT TRACEABILITY
QAS 5010/210	RELATING TO INSTALLATION OF CHEMICAL DAMP-PROOF COURSES
QAS 5020/334	APPLICATION OF MARKING MATERIAL TO RECORD SURFACES & AIRFIELDS.
QAS 5030/1.S	THE INSTALLATION OF UREA FORMALDEHYDE FOAM CAVITY WALL INSULATION.
QAS 5030/345	THE INSTALLATION OF BUILDING ENGINEERING SERVICES
QAS 7902/107	MAINTENANCE OF APPROVED TELECOMMUNICATIONS APPARATUS
QAS 7902/248	WIRING OF TELECOMMUNICATION SYSTEMS OTHER THAN PUBLIC TELECOMUNICATION SYSTEMS
QAS 7902/249	INSTALLATION AND COMMISSIONING OF TELECOMMUNICATION SWITCHING SYSTEMS
QAS 7902/336	MAINTENANCE OF SMALL CALL ROUTING APPARATUS
QAS 7902/337	MAINTENANCE OF LARGE CALL ROUTING APPARATUS
QAS 7902/337	INSTALLATION COMMISSIONING AND CONNECTION OF CALL ROUTING APPARATUS
QAS 7902/381	INSPECTION AND CONNECTION OF INSTALLED CALL ROUTING APPARATUS
QAS 8370/344	DESIGN OF BUILDING ENGINEERING SERVICES
QAS 8370/346	COMMISSIONING OF BUILDING ENGINEERING SERVICES

This list is by no means exhaustive. The Accredited Certification Bodies will be able to advise you on which scheme is best aligned with your company's activity. It should also be noted that some are an extension to BS 5750 Part 1 while others are to Part 2 of the Standard.

QUALITY CIRCLES

The concept of Quality Circles came originally from Japan as a method of refining the local working conditions and improving productivity. I have always seen it as a group form of mini-project management. It is based on two very simple but all too often overlooked factors:

- The staff can often see problems which are not evident to their managers.
- The best people to fix a problem are those who stand to benefit from the solution.

There are only two ground rules which must be rigidly adhered to if a Quality Circle is to be successful. They must restrict themselves to improvements which the department can implement totally within its own resources - this also usually means in practice that it is to be at zero cost. The other rule is, only tackle one problem at a time and this should be the one which yields the highest benefit. They may be highly productive in terms of ideas but some of these should be put on the back-burner for the time being and dealt with one at a time.

The way Quality Circles work is to take a small but representative team from the department; about six is a healthy number to form the Circle. If you have a large department of say 20 staff, then why not form a number of Circles, all working on different areas of the department's activity. A team needs to meet on a regular basis for say no more than half an hour at a time. As a "kick-start" the manager may offer them a very general area of the department's activity to discuss and set them the task of first defining what problems there are, within that area, which they feel are worth fixing.

Their first task then is to brainstorm the subject until they arrive at a short menu of agreed, worthwhile and attainable improvement areas. At this stage they are not required to come up with solutions. This would be foolish, since they haven't really got fully to grips with the problem yet.

The next step, before the next meeting, is for the members of the Quality Circle to think about and perhaps discuss the selected subject with other people in the department and get their views. In essence, they should generally formulate some meaningful opinions.

The next meeting should be another "brainstorming session" to produce three or four good ideas as to what could be done. They will need to allocate some priority to their ideas because, as I said earlier, they should go forward one step at a time but make the first step the most productive one.

The end result should be the implementation of a simple, inexpensive solution to a problem. Now the team can move forward to the next item on their list of objectives. It really is quite amazing how situations which have nagged staff for years can be resolved by this method. An additional spin-off from this kind of activity is that it helps develop team spirit within the department, while giving a nice sense of actually having achieved something practical and worthwhile.

To give you an actual example of the process in practice I recall a Quality Circle looking into the delays they were experiencing getting business expense claims paid. These very often took well over two weeks from the time the staff submitted a claim to the money actually showing up in their bank account.

The Quality Circle tracked through the whole process and found that the major delay was being accumulated in their own department. It was taking almost a week for the secretary to get the claims collected up and signed off by the departmental manager. Added to this the internal mail was taking two days to get the signed forms from the department to the cashier, who was only one floor above them! The remedy was simple and cost nothing to implement.

1.　　A box was placed on the secretary's desk, exclusively for people to drop their expense claims into.
2.　　The manager agreed to always sign off any forms in the box at noon on a Monday.
3.　　The secretary agreed to collect the signed forms from the manager at 13.00 hours every Monday and deliver them, by hand, to the cashier (she passed the cashier on her way to lunch anyway!).
4.　　A short Local Instruction was issued to cover the procedure.
5.　　The secretary's Job Description was amended.

The end result was they halved the delay.

TickIT (ISO 9000-3) - a Sector Scheme for Software

ISO 9000-3 and BS 5750 - Part 13

Following the publication of ISO 9001 in 1987, the Department of Trade and Industry (DTI) wished to establish an equivalent standard to govern the development of software. Two studies were commissioned by the DTI to investigate the methods by which these software packages were developed and make recommendations. The outcome was two papers, one by Price Waterhouse and the other by Logica. The Price Waterhouse conclusions on the costs and benefits of Quality Standards, and the Logica report, which looked into the Quality Management Standards as they might be applied to software, showed great similarities in their findings These two influential reports came up with a number of significant recommendations. Perhaps the two key suggestions were that since the Quality Management Systems required for software had considerable alignment with the rest of the IT industry, then harmonisation with ISO 9001 was probably the best route to take; and guidance would be required to cross-relate the generic ISO 9001 specifications into terms that pertained to the specific processes found in the development of software.

Having accepted these recommendations, the next step for the DTI was to engage the British Computer Society (BCS) to get down to the details of what a software developer should include within its Quality System if it were to gain accreditation as a software developer. The outcome of all this work was TickIT.

Readers with a specific interest in software needing a deeper understanding of the TickIT initiative might care to purchase a copy of *"Guide to Software Quality Management Systems Construction and Certification using EN 29001"* It is available at £7.50 from:

TickIT Project Office,
68 Newman Street,
London W1A 4SE.
Tel: 071-383-4626
Fax: 071-383-4771

Because of the "flexible" nature of software and its capability of being coded and readily configured for a specific application, there need to be clear standards in place which can exert a firm control over its development and ongoing support. It is a reasonable generalisation to say that TickIT can be applied to any organisation where the development of software products and IT systems forms a significant part of its commercial activity.

The range of software available for today's computer systems is immense and yet it is clear to even the casual observer that as the "hardware" grows in both speed and storage capacity then the software, to fully utilise the power of these systems, races to catch up.   The primary aim of TickIT, therefore, is to bring some order and standardisation into a large and still growing sector of the IT industry.

One of the most significant differences between the hardware and the software side of the IT manufacturing sector is that of customer involvement. The makers of hardware, be they large main-frame systems or the desk-top personal computer, are driven by market forces such as price and competitive boxes and the available technology. In the case of hardware the question of *customer needs* is largely taken care of by the diversity of products out there in the marketplace. It is up to the prospective buyer to review what products are available and make his choice. But that choice can be greatly influenced by the available, or potentially available, software systems.

The diversity of custom-developed software packages is, even today, very large . One can find theatre booking systems, library issue control, financial packages, stores inventory management, manufacturing process, sales, electronic mail and so on; I could provide you with pages of specialised software applications. The aim of ISO 9000 - Part 3 (TickIT) is to bring standardisation of the process of developing these customised applications, but more importantly, as I see it, to formally involve the customer (the eventual user) in the creative process.

It should be mentioned that there is now a BSI publication to provide guidance on software, BS 5750 - Part 13, entitled *"Guide to the application of BS 5750 - Part 1 to the development of Software"*. It is available from BSI, priced £38. This new document is in alignment with ISO 9000 - Part 3.

28

A NEW APPROACH

TickIT takes a radically different approach to that of the Quality System model of BS 5750 in a number of ways. One of the first things one notices is the way it has been structured in three major sections (see overleaf).

Quality System - framework

This section defines the requirements as far as the basic infrastructure of the company's Quality System is concerned. It deals with such matters as Management Responsibility and their reviewing of the processes, the Internal Audit Programme and Corrective Action activity and so on.

Quality System - life cycle activities

This focuses on those areas which are most active during the creative, development stages of a project and its support once it is in use by the customer. What is significantly different between BS 5750 - Part 1 and ISO 9000-3 is that in the latter there is a positive requirement during this phase for the "Purchaser" to be a partner in this total process.

Quality System - supporting activities

There are many areas of a company's activity which are "fixed" overheads. They do not in themselves produce an output but without them there would be no end product - or an inferior one at best. Good documentation, tools, training and record keeping, for example, are all essential.

I can visualise the possibility that the ISO 9000-3 model of Quality Assurance, or a derivative, could be readily adapted to any creative venture where the *supplier* is under contract to provide a specific, unique, output for a single *purchaser*. The construction industry might be a suitable example, ship building another. One only needs to examine the clauses of BS 5750 to realise that it is more readlily applied to the repetitive activity of a product manufacturing process or the servicing of equipment than the "one-off" contract where there is a high level of *purchaser* involvment.

Overview of ISO 9000-3

CLAUSE	AREA
1	Scope and field of application
1.1	Scope
1.2	Field of application
2	References - related ISO papers
3	Definitions of certain software terminology
3.1	General definition of "software"
3.2	Additional related definitions
4	*Quality System - framework*
4.1	Management responsibility
4.2	Quality System
4.3	Internal quality system audits
4.4	Corrective action
5	*Quality System - life cycle activities*
5.1	Contract reviews
5.2	Purchaser's requirements specification
5.3	Development planning
5.4	Quality planning
5.5	Design and implementation
5.6	Testing and validation
5.7	Acceptance
5.8	Maintenance
6	*Quality System - supporting activities*
6.1	Configuration management
6.2	Document control
6.3	Quality records
6.4	Measurements
6.5	Rules, practices and conventions
6.6	Tools and techniques
6.7	Purchasing
6.8	Included software products

BS 5750 - Part 1 (1987)

ISO 9001
EN 29001

Narrative

BS 5750 - PART 1 (1987): OVERVIEW

4.1 MANAGEMENT RESPONSIBILITY
Policy defined, resource planning.
Organisation, responsibility and authority.
Verification resources.
Assign management authority.
Review system for effectiveness.

4.2 QUALITY SYSTEM
Documented system to ensure conformity.
Procedures, instructions, etc. in place.

4.3 SERVICE CONTRACT REVIEW
Adequate definition of offering.
Ability to meet contractual agreements.

4.4 DESIGN CONTROL
Verify that design meets specification.
Plans identify aims and responsibilities.
Skills and resource assigned to design.
Managed coordination of the contributors.
Input requirements clearly stated.
Output meets defined requirement.
Verify design as being acceptable.
Control any modifications and re-review.

4.5 DOCUMENTATION CONTROL
Approved and under clear issue control.
Periodic formal reviews for relevancy.
Changes reviewed by owner.
Changes marked so reader can identify.
Documents available to operatives.
Obsolete documents removed/destroyed.

4.6 PURCHASING
Confirm purchase meets specification.
Sub-contractor selected on ability.
Keep records of acceptable sub-contractors.
Quality control by sub-contactor evident.
Purchasing documents clearly state need.
Right to verify conformity of purchase.

4.7 PURCHASER SUPPLIED PRODUCT
Correct storage of materials supplied.
Loss or damage reported to owner.

4.8 PRODUCT IDENTIFICATION AND TRACEABILITY
Reference to drawings, specifications, etc.
Unique identification markings.

4.9 PROCESS CONTROL
Monitoring and control of processes.
Work instructions at all stages.
Criteria of workmanship defined.

4.10 INSPECTION AND TESTING
Incoming material tested or verified.
In process monitoring and testing.
Final testing
Verify all other tests were completed.
Keep all records as evidence of tests.

4.11 INSPECTION, MEASURING AND TEST EQUIPMENT
Establish what equipment is needed.
Identify and label devices and calibrate.
Proper storage, safeguard against misuse.

4.12 INSPECTION AND TEST STATUS
Evidence by means of tags, stamps, marks.

4.13 CONTROL OF NONCONFORMING PRODUCT
Procedures to address defective product.
Firm segregation and clear identification.
Review of cause and possible rework.

4.14 CORRECTIVE ACTION
Define problems and effect lasting solutions
Customer complaints addressed.

4.15 HANDLING, STORAGE, PACKAGING AND DELIVERY
Prevention of damage.
Secure holding area, authorised stock issue.

4.16 QUALITY RECORDS
Identification, collection, filing and storage.
Records held to demonstrate achievement.
Retention times established and recorded.

4.17 INTERNAL QUALITY AUDITS
Planned and documented.
Scheduled on basis of importance.
Documented evidence of corrective actions.

4.18 TRAINING
Identification of needs.
Provision of training and evaluation.
Records available of training received.

4.19 SERVICING
Reviewed against contractual undertaking.
Performance statistics available.

4.20 STATISTICAL TECHNIQUES
Verification of performance.
Review of performance against targets.

MANAGEMENT RESPONSIBILITY

COMMITMENT - FROM THE TOP DOWN

The Standard sets out by clearly placing the responsibility for the Quality System firmly in the hands of company management. Unless the commitment is evident at the top of the management chain, there is only a minimum chance that the system will ever take root. The Standard asks three things of senior management; to *declare*, *define*, and *document* its commitment to its aims, as follows:

Declare its total commitment to the Quality System. This could take many forms but I would strongly recommend a letter from the head of the organisation to each employee stating the senior management's pledge to the Quality Policy of the company. Furthermore, a copy of this letter should be the very first page of the Quality Manual. I have provided an example of such a letter as the first page of the sample Quality Manual in Part 2 of this book.

Define the company policy regarding Quality. The company Quality Manual springs out of this requirement, since if you look carefully at the terms of the Quality Manual in Part 2 you will see that it mainly states *what* rather than *how*. In practice, once the policy has been clearly defined and unambiguously stated in the Quality Manual it seldom needs to be modified. The Quality System itself, however, may undergo constant revision as the company develops and modifies its operational practices.

Document, inasmuch as the senior manager, usually the Managing Director, should be the "owner" of the Quality System and consequently the Quality Manual. The Quality Manual should specify in broad terms the adoption of BS 5750 to match the specific requirements of your company. I have provided, in Part 2, a Sample Quality Manual which you may care to adapt to your own company's needs. I would normally expect to find that the Managing Director will have delegated the actual administration of the process and the top level documents to someone such as the Quality Manager. In overall terms the Standard expects that every process and procedure which contributes to the Quality of your company's output has been clearly documented (See Topic 4.5).

REVIEWING AND MONITORING

The appointment of a Quality Manager will allow senior management to delegate the day-to-day running of the Quality System but it does not absolve them of the overall responsibility for its success or (the unthinkable) its failure. The Standard requires that management, and I think we have to mean the top management, review at sensible intervals the overall performance of their company within the Quality System. I would, as an outside inspector, expect to find evidence that at least once a year, but in the early stages perhaps twice, a formal *Quality System Review* meeting of senior managers taking place. This meeting should have as an absolute minimum the following items on its agenda:

1. The results of the Quality Audit Programme for the preceding twelve (or six) months.
2. Surveillance reports by the accreditation body.
3. Statistical performance and customer perception.
4. Expansion and/or improvements to the Quality System.

PROMOTION OF QUALITY

Over and above the quite specific mandatory duties, the senior management team could do much more to further the cause of Quality. The following menu of ideas should be seen as ways to indicate the company's continuing commitment to the pursuit of Quality. The following eleven proposals could be addressed at the Quality System Review.

LAUNCH MEETING

Have a "kick-off" meeting where the senior management team take the opportunity to stress the top-to-bottom commitment to the scheme. They could, at this time introduce the Quality Manager, who could run through a short presentation of how the company intend to work within the conditions of the Standard. But if you take up this idea then make sure it's done with style. Use the best speakers you can obtain; if need be consider a well known professional to provide polish and continuity to the event. Don't skimp on visual aids, make them good and to a standard quality format. Remember as you plan the launch that you are selling *Quality* and so this is to be the one business meeting which must have *class* and not fade from the minds of the company employees.

QUALITY VIDEO

It will depend on the size of your company, but it may not be practical to bring everyone in for a launch presentation. A well made video may be the solution, but again, don't skimp - remember a well made video can have a powerful and lasting impact. One further advantage of the video is that it could be used over and over again to introduce new members of the company to your commitment to Quality. There is also the option that the video could be the first item on the programme at the launch presentation, as a scene-setter.

QUALITY STATEMENT

I have mentioned earlier that a Statement of Quality Policy from the head of the company is required and that a letter spelling this out is virtually mandatory. However, sending it out, getting it read, and more importantly getting it etched in the mind is a tall order to expect from one sheet of paper. A more durable method of placing the message before the staff, which I have seen successfully adopted, is to provide each manager with a simple but neatly framed copy of the Statement, which could be hung in some prominent position in the department.

QUALITY AWARDS

I like the idea of maintaining some focus by initiating an Awards scheme which would incorporate the formal recognition of the contribution of some member of staff, perhaps on a monthly basis. It is not difficult for the Quality Department, who see right across the various departments, to spot someone who has demonstrated the principle of Quality in some special and individualistic way.

NEW HIRE INDUCTION

So often the big message of Quality is announced to the current team of employees at the time of the launch and then the package is put in a bottom drawer, never to be seen again. Unless you have a totally fixed work force in a company that never grows then you are constantly bringing in new people and they need to understand your commitment to Quality. The best time to start doing this is the second they walk through your door on the day they join. This is supposing the cause of Quality had not been apparent at the time of their interview for the job in the first place. The section of their initial training where they get to know all those important things, like the size and diversity of your organisation and how the senior management is structured, is a perfect time to introduce them to the Quality Policy. I would suggest you should use the most senior manager you can muster to present the concept to the new people so that they know from the start of their careers with your company that Quality is a top-management-driven discipline.

QUALITY BULLETIN

I know that many companies perhaps publish and distribute too many "newsletter" types of publication and they begin to lose their impact. Nevertheless, something exclusively focused on the company's drive on Quality might serve as a reminder periodically that Quality was not just the flavour of the month when it was introduced. It would serve to demonstrate that it is an ongoing campaign. One low-cost solution might be to add a supplement to some other widely distributed house magazine. There are generally plenty of substantial topics which can be quoted to demonstrate improving Quality, such as simple statistical diagrams showing items like reducing customer complaints, customer satisfaction survey results, improving response time to customer requests for service. Most of this information is readily available at senior management level and would take very little effort to prepare it for a wider audience. Just as they might take pride in the parameters which show a constant line of improvement, the employees need to know when the charts are going the other way. You will find that to broadcast to the staff that there is a disturbing trend downwards in some parameter or another is all that is needed to effect the desired reverse trend.

QUALITY NOTICE-BOARD

An alternative to the bulletin or newsletter idea might be an attractive dedicated notice-board in some prominent position which will catch the eye and attention of everyone (including visitors). This could be used to show off a few key top-level statistics and perhaps photographs and citations of award winners.

QUALITY POSTERS

A few well designed posters around the company premises can, if they are thoughtfully and creatively designed, be a helpful reminder. Don't, I beg you, put up a first issue and leave it there to grow old and yellow. The trick of advertising is to get your public awaiting the next poster. If you don't believe me, think of the "Benson & Hedges" series with their semi-disguised packets. Also remember that just because Quality in itself is a serious topic doesn't mean humour should be excluded.

HOUSE STYLE

I feel that an identifiable logo and house style should be associated with the Quality System and once established it should be rigidly adhered to. I would point out that the best logos I have ever seen arrest the attention because of their simplicity.

MEMENTOS

A small selection of inexpensive but useful items such as letter openers, perennial calendars etc, are always handy to distribute to both customers and staff. Since these items are intended to show your company's lasting association with Quality, avoid the cheap and eventually useless things like clocks that need batteries you can't obtain, or key rings that rust the first time they see a spot of rain.

ADVERTISING

Once you have Registration then make use of it. Permission will have to be sought from the accreditation body which granted the registration, or BSI to make use of their Quality Assurance logo, but generally this is always granted since it helps promote the cause of BS 5750 itself just as much as it does your company.

QUALITY SYSTEM

THREE BASIC REQUIREMENTS

The basic requirements are that you first prepare a documented system which covers all aspects of your company's Quality procedures and instructions; second that you put what you have decided as being your company's Quality System into practice; and finally you must be able to demonstrate that you are maintaining your overall Quality Policy by both monitoring its application and improving the scheme by frequent constructive reviews.

QUALITY POLICY

The first step of this path is to set out carefully your Policy as to Quality across the various departments of the company and from that consideration you should be able to produce a *Quality Manual* (see Part 2). This need not be a massive tome; it needs only to paraphrase the Standard in terms which tailor it to your company and its needs. Once it is published and distributed it should need very little, if any, modification or alteration, providing you are careful not to include too much detail but keep it more as a statement of policy.

QUALITY PROCEDURES

The various Procedures, both company-wide and departmental, are where most of the change activity will take place. I mention two levels of Procedures since many of the procedures which are followed in a company are of a wide general nature and affect most, if not all, departments. I would cite the purchasing of materials and services from an outside source as perhaps a good example. Here we would expect the Purchasing Department to specify the rules and conditions that any other section of the company would have to follow should they need to make outside purchases. This would be a typical example of just one company-wide Quality Procedure.

DEPARTMENTAL PROCEDURES

You should give all departmental managers the opportunity to write their own relevant Procedures. It makes a great deal of sense since many will already have the substance of such procedures already in place and will only need to make a few cosmetic adjustments. Almost certainly there will be some practices which have never been defined to the point of writing down

41

instructions to cover them. A good guide is to pose the question - should we have a procedure? Does the process under consideration have any relevance at all to the "output" of the company. For example, I would suggest that the procedure by which an employee books their vacation doesn't, but the periodical upgrading of a control programme across a network of terminals might well qualify.

WORK INSTRUCTION

If any task being carried out by the company staff could, if not executed correctly, result in a compromise in terms of Quality, then there should be a Work Instruction to guide them through the steps. You may feel a documented Work Instruction to be somewhat insulting to your people if the task is so simple and straightforward that it is self-evident as to how to carry it out. But be careful, test your belief and ask, "If a new-comer to the company were given the task in question, could they carry it out without error?" I think you would find very frequently the answer to be that they couldn't. We will return to the subject of Work Instructions when we look at Process Control in Topic 4.9.

QUALITY REVIEWS

Your Quality System should not be static - business certainly isn't. There has to be a process to formally review the total system at regular intervals, say every 6 months or so. I described in the previous Topic how there is a requirement in the Standard for a formal review by Senior Management. There is an additional process which many companies find effective which I will call *Quality Reviews*. The object of these meetings is to get together those members of staff who are actually conducting the Internal Quality Audit programme and pool their joint experience. The primary aim would be to look for common weaknesses across the company, enhance the auditing process and decide on key areas to monitor during the next phase of Internal Audits. A typical agenda for such a Quality Review might include:

- Internal Audit programme - last period (say last 3 months).
- Internal Audit Programme - next period, plan and allocate auditors.
- Auditor training.
- Outstanding Concessions (temporary permitted deviations).
- Surveillance activity by the accreditation body.
- Outstanding Corrective Actions.
- Quality documentation.

The "minutes" from these Quality Reviews could usefully form the basis of the Quality Manager's report to the senior management team and then used as part of their own Quality System Review (see Topic 4.1).

IMPROVEMENTS

This clause of the standard also expects a company to be constantly striving for better ways of carrying out its creative processes. You will be expected to be looking for improvements in your tests as you learn more about your product line and to spot any inherent weakness in design. Better manufacturing techniques, superior materials and components all are part of BS 5750. A company's Research and Development is a key factor in the overall quest for Product Quality and consequently should be a documented and controlled function within the system.

CONTRACT REVIEW

INTRODUCTION

Contract Review refers to any signed agreement you have with your customers or suppliers. It should embrace both the supply of goods and any service contract your company has entered into with the customer. Furthermore, in the case of a maintenance or repair service it should include a review of the offering, and any possible change when the contract comes round to its annual renewal. For the sake of clarity I will discuss the various types of contract separately.

CONTRACT REVIEW - SERVICE

In most companies the Service Contracts for the maintenance of electronic equipment are renewable annually and it surprises me how frequently I see such contracts being "renewed" with no rc-cvaluation of the service levels provided or the inventory of equipment included in the contract.

In the cases where some form of review takes place the customer is frequently by-passed. Contract review by the supplier of the service might be allowed to assume, in the absence of any instruction by the customer, that the hours of cover to be provided will remain as it had been during the previous 12 month period. But experience tells me that the physical inventory installed at the customer's premises is very likely to change. So some correlation needs to be made between the equipment shown on the contract schedule and the actual equipment at the customer's site. Your own records will be be able to list any new equipment that has been shipped on site in the previous 12 months, if you happen to be the supplier as well as the maintainer. The problem is the equipment shipped in by the customer from other sources. It is common these days for the larger national companies to transfer terminals, modems, personal computers and even small mainframe systems between their various sites. The only real answer to this problem is to carry out some form of physical "on-site" inventory check of your own once a year. It is generally quite simple for an engineer to conduct such a check when on a service call.

The opportunity for the Sales Representative to visit a customer at the time of the annual contract review shouldn't be passed up. Bear in mind that you may be in a "win" situation. You may be the bearer of good news in that his current maintenance costs are to be reduced. This may leave him in a surplus revenue situation which may be convertible into the purchase of additional

45

services from your company. On the other hand, the combined effect of your inventory check on his installation and any increase in your basic charges you are introducing may result in an increase. Such news needs something more than an impersonal form letter from your billing department - at the minimum a presentation to the customer of the facts by the responsible sales person is called for.

There are many parameters within the terms of a service contract that may be subject to variation, other than the actual costs. Your procedures for reviewing service contracts should acknowledge such factors as response time, routine maintenance, on-site spares, remote service support, hours of cover, etc. An enhancement of some of these parameters may cost your company very little and yet may be very desirable to your customer and more than compensate for a slight increase in the monthly cost for maintenance cover.

I may have strayed away from my brief slightly in that BS 5750 does not specify the manner of these reviews, only that the supplier and the customer should be seen to interface appropriately. One final point, however; the Standard does require that you keep records of these contract reviews, so there's another reason for doing them!

ONE-TIME SERVICE CONTRACT (Task)

I use the term "one-time" to describe a situation where you are required to carry out a single, but often large, contractual undertaking, such as installing a Local Area Network, or maybe wiring up the 2000 extensions needed in a new building for the telephone system.

The starting point has to be a carefully formulated Procedure which, if followed by your people, will ensure that your company doesn't take on a task which it is either unable to fulfil to the satisfaction of the customer or, as quite often happens, can only be completed by your company making a financial loss! This Procedure is hopefully going to steer the activity for many contracts in the future and so it is worthwhile making a substantial initial investment of your time to get the process wide in its application and yet firm in its disciplines.

Take the case of wiring a new building as a sample to illustrate the stages needed to arrive at a "Contract". Many customers at the early stage of a project may have only a limited technical knowledge of the required task and so to ask them to define it would be pointless. For this reason you may find that in practice, the definition will come out of the site survey by your own staff. Nevertheless, I believe it is the customer who should be responsible for defining his own requirements.

What is difficult to deal with in practice is the pressure to virtually provide the customer with a "design service" for free. Naturally you want to win the contract and the prospective customer may not have the expertise to carry out the design work for himself. You have to tread a thin line between providing enough assistance to win the contract, while not providing the customer with enough information for him to say "Thank you" and take what you have provided for free, and do the work himself with the aid of some locally hired contractors.

One possible answer to this predicament is to divide your contract into four distinct elements:

- *Provisional Design Proposal.* This would be a "free" but limited facility to draft out a proposed design. I would highlight what you were proposing in principle but would stop short of any drawings or material listings. It might, for example, provide the prospective customer with one site visit to review the task. Collect any supporting information that might be relevant, for example drawings of the site, what trunking and underfloor ducting is there in place, and so on. You might then create a basic draft proposal with an estimate of the cost. If the customer is suitably impressed then he may elect to sign a contract for full Design Service.

- *Design Service .* Many customers may at the outset of a project have the view that they could save costs if they were to carry out the physical work themselves but recognise that they may not have the technical knowledge to design the requirement in-house. This route has the additional bonus from the customer's point of view that if he runs into any difficulties in the implementation stages then he can call on your company to diagnose the problem, since he had installed to *your* design.

- *Consultancy.* Since we are discussing large-scale, frequently complex technical considerations, it may be that the customers wish to buy the service of an expert in the field, rather than risk going it alone. This way they can get the best of both worlds. They will obtain a design tailored to their requirements and the professional management to see it through to completion.

- *Installation.* Most customers will generally opt for an outside agency to carry out the actual installation work. It's a specialised undertaking that calls for concerted effort over a relatively short period of time. This physical work may also need to be done outside business hours, which can compound the problems.

So, to return to the overall topic of Contract Review. What is required is a Procedure which clearly describes the options which are available, and how we intend to review that what we undertook to supply is indeed being supplied. The Procedure should include parameters for all the various forms of contracts entered into with your customers.

The Procedure might follow along the lines of the sequence I have listed below. It should also specify who has direct responsibility for each step, as I have done. The advantage of drawing up a table such as this is to ensure that not only does every step in the process below get covered but that there is a clear definition of who is responsible for each phase.

Task	Responsibility
Overall management responsibility	Sales
Customer's definition of need	Customer/Sales/Engineering
Survey of site	Engineering
Draft proposal	Engineering
Adjustments	Customer/Engineering
Budgetary estimate	Purchasing
Detailed plan	Engineering
Cost estimate	Purchasing
Manpower available	Engineering
Produce the contract	Administration
Produce the schedule	Administration
Schedule to customer	Sales
Contract to customer	Sales
Customer signature	Sales
Purchase materials	Purchasing
Work	Engineering
Completion	Engineering
Billing	Administration
Post mortem review	All

How well are the terms and conditions of the contract defined? By "defined" I mean fully documented, with evidence that the "purchaser" is in agreement.

The "purchaser's specifications" may well be adequate as they stand and a reference to, and copy of, such a customer specification may well be sufficient, if available. However, if there is an agreed deviation from the customer's design or specification, then this must be clearly defined and documented. Take care that your Procedures address the need to investigate carefully the full implications of any deviations from the specifications. It might turn out that just a minor alteration to a characteristic in one area of a product may have a major consequential impact in some other.

BS 5750 calls for the apparently simplistic need that the supplier is capable of meeting the contractual requirement. I have seen a situation where the contract actually agreed to a functional operating test for an item of equipment under a quite specific range of temperatures. Yet, on careful inspection, the thermostatic controllers on the manufacturer's testing ovens were not designed to hold a regulated temperature at the top end of the required range. So how could they have ever met the contractual agreement they had entered into?

Have a look at the Service Contract Review section of the New Era plc Quality Manual (Part 2 Section 4.3), which may give you further food for thought.

DESIGN CONTROL

HARDWARE, SOFTWARE OR SERVICES

The word Design, in the context of BS 5750, applies equally to whatever marketable output your company is offering to its customers. It would be a serious mistake to imagine that it refers only to the design of physical objects. More frequently these days it is the servicing of equipment that is being supplied and Clause 4.4 of BS 5750 will equally embrace this activity. And let us not forget the growing industry of custom-built software packages.

Step one is clearly to define responsibility for each of the various stages of the planning and design. I will restrict my discussion to that of a "service offering", since this is a common, but least understood, area of application of BS 5750. In principle the steps to be taken are much the same as would be the case for, say, a piece of hardware or custom-built software application.

DESIGN AND DEVELOPMENT PLANNING

The design activity for a service offering may not be a full-time task, in fact it is very unlikely to be so. But the person entrusted with this function needs to have quite clear objectives, adequate resources available to him and equally important, authority across many departments of the organisation. This is essential since he may have to reconcile objections and deviations to the design by the various participating departments.

Let's not overlook the customer who may have some input we should consider. It is surprising how a company will spend millions in detailed market research to establish exactly what will sell in the case of a solid piece of exciting new hardware, but then leave the after sales servicing element as an internal matter. More enlightened companies will see the servicing just as much a part of the attraction of the total product package as the hardware and software.

So, who inside the company needs to have a say? Well, this will to some extent depend on how the service is to be delivered. Quite possibly you may be considering using a third party organisation to deliver some or all of the service element. Every company will be slightly different, but I feel each of the following groups might have some useful input:

51

Field Engineering   Stores

Product Design   Purchasing

Subcontractor   Legal

Training   Marketing

Whenever possible the management of the Design should be invested in someone responsible for the delivery of the service, such as Engineering. One of their first tasks will be to assign sub-responsibilities and establish lines of communication. A target launch date should be set and agreed, and from that a series of regular progress/review meetings can be scheduled. These should be formal, well structured occasions where any conflicting interests are resolved. BS 5750 also requires that these meetings are documented and circulated to all interested parties. The actual word the Standard uses is "transmitted", but I feel we can take this to mean "circulated".

DESIGN INPUT

The principle aim of design input is to make sure that what we want from the product (in our case a service offering) has been adequately specified at the outset. The design input should embrace every aspect of the requirement and give consideration to the factors and parameters that the service is to meet, once it becomes part of the business. As mentioned in the previous paragraph, regular meetings should be held to ensure the design considerations are being totally observed. The list shown below gives you some idea of the scale of the agenda and I'm sure you could add to it:

Warranty   Parts availability

Staffing levels and training Levels of service

Service contract hours   Response times

Service support and technical Tools and test equipment
 back-up   needed

24 Hour availability   Offsite diagnostics

Call receipt and despatch   Mean time between failures

DESIGN OUTPUT

In our sample, where we are considering a Service Contract as the output, we can express the design output in very precise terms, something along the lines of the contract shown overleaf.

52

1.   *This Service Contract will be available to any client with the
        New Era Processor - Model 4003.*

2.   *The contract is available in four modes:*
        Silver: *8-hour response, business hours*
        Gold: *4-hour response, business hours*
        Premium: *4 hours response round the clock*
        Standard: *24 hours response 08.30 to 18.00
                        (Monday to Friday inclusive).*

3.   *Cancellation of contract by either party requires one
        month's notice.*

4.   *Business hours Help Desk for all Service Contract
        holders*

5.   *Technical Performance and Safety Improvements
        developed by New Era plc will be fitted free of charge.*

6   *Terms and conditions of the contract to be reviewed
        annually.*

A sample Service Contract

You might elect to include in the contract a few other items of information, such as the percentage in monthly charge if they wish to extend the hours of cover (except "Premium", which is round the clock anyway). You will also notice that I haven't, in the above six terms, given the customer any pledge as to what I will do if I fail to meet the contractual response times. A possibility which might gain you some advantage over the competition could be to offer a discount if it falls, say, below 95%. I'm sure you would agree that it would be unthinkable were your local supermarket allowed to get away with selling bags of *roundabout* 1kg of sugar, so why should the service industry be any different?

To their credit, British Telecom are now giving their customers reductions in the monthly bill if they, BT, fail to restore the service within a specified timescale following a fault being reported to them.

DESIGN VERIFICATION

The Standard quite reasonably expects that your company will, following the launch of a service, carry out planned reviews to establish that what you are providing is what you set out to provide. Reliable evidence in the form of verifiable performance figures, coupled to an intelligent application of statistical analysis, should be seen to be the backbone of such a review. I would be additionally impressed if it were evident that the customer's opinion formed some part of this review. Were I auditing such a review, I would hope to find continuity in the people attending right through, from the early design stages to the post-launch review.

DESIGN CHANGES

A perfectly good design can be ruined by random, uncontrolled changes. If you have put so much effort into the original design, verifying each step of the way, then subject any alterations to the same stringent rules. Changes are intended to be for the betterment of the design and therefore they should be encouraged, but make the design team prove it. In summary, what the Standard asks is that:

- Appropriate approval is obtained
- Changes are carried out in a controlled manner
- The effects of the changes are carefully evaluated
- The changes are fully documented

DOCUMENTATION

INTRODUCTION

A great deal of thought needs to go into the structure of the documentation within a Quality System. The major errors I see time and time again are too much documentation, poorly designed with no firm control of the distribution. You can add to these sins a fourth - documenting what you would like to happen, rather than what is happening. The things you have to get right from the start are:

- *Structure.* I mean the overall basic structure (see the overview on the last page of this Topic) within which any documents, and by documents we generally mean books, manuals, or forms, are arranged. Good structure will keep the documents to a minimum while reducing overlapping and duplication.

- *Design.* A uniform, distinctive yet simple "house style", and I put the emphasis on the word "simple". For example, don't clutter the pages up with fancy logo, borders and motifs.

- *Distribution.* You will need to develop a manageable process by which you can, with the minimum disruption, inconvenience and cost, keep the information current and distributed to the people who need it to carry out their duties.

DOCUMENT CHANGES

You'll need to put in place strict rules of "amendment". A documentation system which over-restricts amendments will rapidly fall into disuse; it has to be able to develop so that it clearly reflects the workings of the company. Sections will need to be reissued from from time to time to keep abreast of current techniques and procedures. The documents which are to be used by a large population of your company need to be under strict rules of amendment. It follows, therefore that someone is going to have to review and update the contents, and this should be the registered owner. Nevertheless, anyone who uses the documents should be allowed to suggest amendments to the owner and I have included a form (Q0502; see Part 3, *p. 192*) for this purpose.

The documentation change process is illustrated overleaf.

55

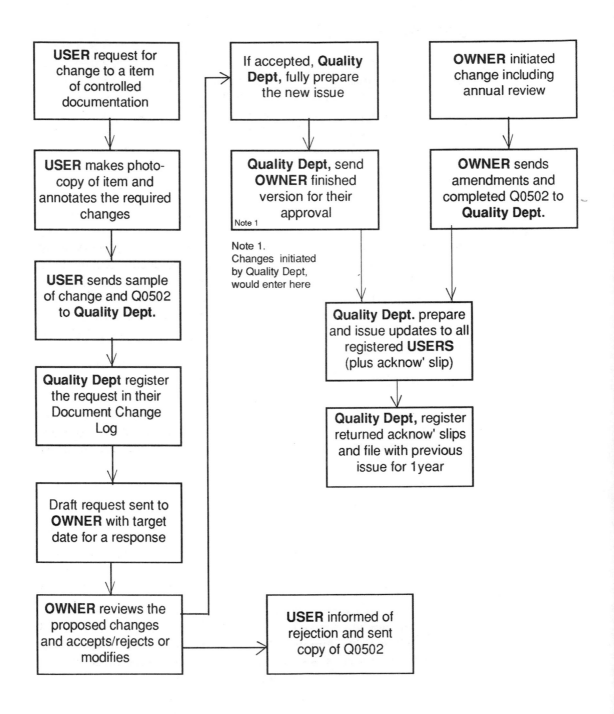

Documentation Change Process

OWNERSHIP

The next point to consider is the "Ownership" of specific documents. The ownership of a document should be a department or function, such as the Stores Manager or Chief Buyer, and not the individual by name. You will save your company a great deal of re-issuing by avoiding proper names. People change posts generally more frequently than procedures require modification and hence re-issue. You could if you wish add a page somewhere at the front of the manual, perhaps even on the amendment sheet, which equates Owner to a named person but this isn't really necessary.

The sub-division of the documentation and structuring it into definitive sections will save you a lot of work when it comes to changing it at some later date. I've seen Procedures Manuals where a change to one manufacturing process required the entire manual to be re-issued because the structure of the page numbering couldn't accommodate the inclusion of an additional page.

I believe that every manual should have a small quantity of change request forms (Q0502) at the back of the book so the users can formally bring about improvements.

DOCUMENTATION CHANGE CONTROL

Whatever department has responsibility for the distribution of a Manual (and I would suggest this should be the Quality Department), then it logically follows that they need to know who has each copy so they know to whom they must send the amendment.

AMENDMENT SHEET

An important aspect of any Quality volume of documentation is to be able to discover quickly whether or not what you are reading is up to date. I've seen many ways of trying to do this, and the solution is whatever is best for your own documentation structure. This book you are reading has been produced with a form of documentation control and an amendments system (although naturally we will not be sending you updated material through the post), but it can serve a useful purpose if only to demonstrate a method which covers all the requirements, and you may find it adaptable to your needs.

DOCUMENT AND PAGE NUMBERING

You wouldn't think that such a simple topic required a section to itself, but don't you believe it. I have seen methods used which have ended up as millstones around the neck, making the most minor amendments a costly time-consuming business. Let us firstly consider a flexible yet logical approach to giving each document a unique identifier. The Quality Manual isn't a problem, since there is only one definitive volume and it generally doesn't often get changed, but Procedures are quite another matter. You are likely to have many company-wide procedures described in your documentation, and each department will have a set of procedures pertaining to its own particular needs. You will see that in the examples I have included in this book, I have simply given each Procedure, Work Instruction, and so on, a title followed by a two digit identification number and, below that a description of the activity it relates to, as shown in the diagram below.

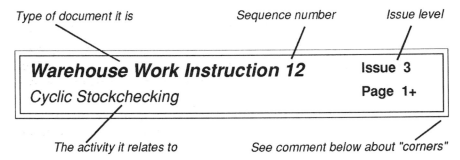

Information needed in headings on Quality Documentation

It is helpful, I find, if one can, at a glance, distinguish between local documents and those issued company-wide, such as the Quality Manual. I have illustrated in the above example one simple way of doing this; square corners on the "banner" means it's a local document, while round corners indicate company-wide distribution.

As for page numbering, don't make the mistake of numbering a manual sequentially from cover to cover. I have seen it done, and every time a topic needed to be expanded, the whole book had to be reissued. The answer is simple; number the pages sequentially but limited within each procedure. Then, at the worst, all you will need to send out when you make some amendment would be that single procedure. Better yet, note how the page numbering has been arranged in the page "header" information of this book *(See p. 7)*.

ISSUE STATUS

It is essential that users of a manual should be able to determine for themselves if the copy they are using is the latest issue. The Issue Control Matrix is one solution to this problem. Have a look at the Issue Control Matrix provided with the Quality Manual in Part 2 *(p. 141)*. This enables you to establish whether you are looking at a fully maintained version or not. I have included a blank Issue Control Matrix within Part 3 which you might choose to adopt *(see p. 191)*.

FORMS

All administration systems require "forms" of some sort and in this respect a Quality System is no exception. This section aims both to arm you with a few basic ground rules regarding the design of forms and provide you with a small set of essential forms (see Part 3) which could be incorporated into your system, perhaps with some customisation.

Forms are a very important and visible part of any Quality System, so don't skimp on their design. The credibility of the whole process could be jeopardised if they look cheap or fussy or difficult to use. Try to maintain one standard size for all your forms, preferably A4 since it makes for more straightforward photocopying, and will match up to most filing systems. You may notice that the forms I have included are not A4 because of the actual size of this book, but they could be enlarged.

Keep the artwork to an absolute minimum. You will notice in the samples provided, that I have established a "header" without any fancy text style or special logo. Each form provides you, in the header, with the only three things you need to know - its purpose, identification number and issue status.

Endeavour to get a "flow" to your forms by placing required information in logical blocks. Have a look at the form Q0502 I have provided in Part 3 *(p. 192)*, called Document Change Request; this is a good example of what I mean. The first block asks you to define exactly *what* you want to have changed. The second block provides you with some space to detail *how* you want it changed. It then requires information as to *who* is asking. Then we have a block to establish the agreement to the change by the "owner" of the form, and finally a panel to close off the action.

If there is a need for some special identification information, such as there is on form Q0502, i.e. the *Document Change Number*, then place it in a standard area of the form (top right hand corner is a good place) and put a box round it to draw it to the user's attention. All the forms in the system should be approved and registered by the Quality Department and they should hold ← a copy of every registered form in their Master Library .

Another thing about the design of forms - don't ask for information that you really don't require just to fill up the space on the page.

Multi-purpose forms can have their uses but I feel, in a Quality System, they should be avoided. Your rule should be - the simpler the form, the better.

Provide the user with some guidance notes within the form if you really think it will help, but avoid cluttering up the sheet. If you feel that completing the form calls for clarification, then point the users to a Procedure in the documentation which will give them chapter and verse on how they should be filling in the various sections.

Each form needs to be allocated an unique identification number, and I have seen some very complex and bizarre systems in my time. You should give a great deal of thought to this matter and arrive at a format which produces relatively short identifiers which are still flexible and expandable enough to deal with additions and deletions. The forms I have provided follow the following simple format. The leading letter indicates the department (of New Era plc) that actually owns the form, as shown below:

Q = Quality	D = Development and Design	L = Logistics
P = Production	M = Marketing	E = Engineering

Of the four digits following the letter the first two indicate the related clause of BS 5750. The remaining two digits are simply a serial number. For example an E1901 is the form used by Engineering (**E**) to record a Service Request (Servicing is clause 4.**19** of the Standard) and the **01** is a serial number. Whatever method you finally decide to use, keep it simple and flexible and don't permit anyone to deviate from the scheme.

ELECTRONIC DOCUMENTATION

If your company has some form of electronic mail then I would strongly recommend you look into the possibility of building your Quality documentation onto it. The advantages are many, for one thing it completely eliminates the distribution problems of paper and makes your photocopiers last longer.

Another key gain is that everyone has immediate access to the very latest version of every item. Most electronic mail systems have the capability of holding partition libraries of "read only" material. I've seen this facility frequently used as a kind of notice-board. I would strongly suggest that you investigate the possibility of using this capability to hold the Quality Manual and the top level Quality Procedures. I used an "on-line" mail system myself for the first Quality System I developed in the mid-seventies and the advantages over paper are enormous. For one thing it reduced the "hard-copy" requirement by about 80% and that was a lot of photocopying. But the real advantage is it virtually eliminates the updating and distributing problems, since there is only one copy of all the major manuals and I was keeping that up-to-date from my office terminal. I took the system down to the level of Work Instructions and small Local Procedures and it was a very powerful aid.

The value of such a system was that when one of my staff was about to carry out some activity he hadn't done for some time, he simply went on-line, found the Work Instruction he needed and printed it out all fresh and at the current issue level. As a safeguard against old "hard-copy" versions being used over and over again, I programmed the library to enter the following line at the top of any print-out taken:

> THIS IS A **REFERENCE ONLY COPY** PRINTED ON 12/05/89

A further refinement worth mentioning was to pass the *ownership* of certain items of the documentation to my staff to keep up to date. The way this worked was that if an owner needed to update the on-line content of his particular document, he would first take an electronic copy down onto his own disk storage. Electronic Mail systems always provide the user with a few sectors of disk as a work area. Once he had the document in his work area he could make whatever alterations were needed. He would then electronically mail the document to me, just as if it were a piece of mail. I would see if I was happy with the changes and, if I was, I would replace the old version with this up-to-date one.

You might wonder why the *owner* didn't take this last step himself. The answer is simple. The documents were made "read only" as far as my staff were concerned. Only I could action any changes to the actual "library". This way we were protected against someone going into a document and introducing errors in the text.

The Quality Manual should describe, in broad terms, the overall adaptation of BS 5750 to the working environment of your company. It needs to describe how each applicable clause of the Standard is to be implemented. It should also establish the structure, authority and responsibility for the maintenance of the company Quality System. It should describe *what* happens rather than *how*, and hence rarely needs changing.

Quality Procedures should contain clear, detailed descriptions of those processes which are common across all, or most, departments of the company. These might include such functions as Quality Auditing, Documentation and its control, Training, Contract Reviews and Customer-compliant handling, etc.

Department Procedures are those which are applicable to specific areas of the company activity. For example, the Calibration procedure for test equipment need only be available in the Department Procedures Manual for Engineering, whereas the Procedure for the safe handling of electrostatically sensitive circuitry may need to be available to some departments but not all. A decision will sometimes need to be made as to whether a Procedure might be better placed in the Quality Procedures Manual and therefore be available across all departments.

Local Procedures provide a means by which each working unit can describe how certain parochial requirements should be carried out. An example might be the procedure by which a Service Engineer can obtain spare parts outside normal working hours, or how data on a hard-disk should be backed up each evening. Local Procedures should be produced, maintained and distributed by the "owning" department manager, but I would strongly recommend that the Quality Department are on the distribution list.

Work Instructions, as their title suggests, provide a means by which a manager can describe exactly how some function within his authority should be carried out. Here I would cite such operations as giving an item of equipment its periodic maintenance or how to carry out a "cyclic" stock check in a stores. Once again, as with Local Procedures, any Work Instruction needs to be constantly reviewed to ensure it's accurate and describes the optimum way to carry out the task.

Quality Documentation: an overview

PURCHASING

BUYER BEWARE

The materials and services that your company purchases to form part of your own marketable product need to be subjected to the same vigorous conditions of quality you impose on your own output.

At first sight this might appear to be self-evident, yet many companies are quite weak in this area of the Standard. Frequently, in these days of modular production, a finished product is nothing more than the result of bringing together any number of sub-assemblies built by various subcontractors. It follows therefore that if your customer believes he is purchasing a Quality product then much of that quality is in the hands of others.

For this reason purchasing comes very high in the ranking of major functions when considering the issue of quality. All companies involve themselves in the purchasing of either materials or services or both. The general aim of this clause of the Standard is to ensure that what you purchase conforms to the specification which you defined to your supplier or subcontractor. This presupposes that you have indeed defined in unambiguous terms exactly what you wish them to supply.

Having defined our needs, the next question is "How do you know they are totally satisfying them?"

Before starting to lay down any ground rules we need to consider *what* we are purchasing. We could be talking about components straight from the supplier's catalogue: - resistors, capacitors, bulbs, etc. At this end of the range of purchasing you usually have the opportunity to quickly change suppliers if, by sample testing, the items don't consistently meet your requirement. But let me tell you a story which I know from first-hand experience to be true and may give you pause for thought in respect to small insignificant items of "supply". A large manufacturer had, within one of their major products, racks full of identical electronic circuit boards. On these circuit boards were some bulky wire wound resistors. They were bulky and well ventilated because, if a certain plug-in device external to the machine, but connected to the board via plug and socket, ever developed a fault, this resistor drew a great deal of current and became quite hot. To provide good ventilation the resistors were mounted on ceramic pillars holding them clear of the circuit board. The subcontractor assembling the circuit boards either didn't have it specified to him or didn't realise the possible consequence, but he switched to using nylon (inflammable!)

pillars. The end result was a fire in one installation that completely destroyed a £300,000 machine. Further costs were incurred as many expensive man-hours were deployed going around the country finding and removing the rest of these potentially hazardous items.

The moral is - *specify exactly* what you want and then *check frequently* to ensure that you are getting it!

Reference to the topic of "Purchasing" isn't limited to that of physical articles; don't forget services. There are many sub-services your company purchases which can directly affect the overall Quality of your output, for example, transport services to get spares delivered to your field engineers out at customer sites, or a calibration service for your test equipment, even the software to drive your product may have been designed out and purchased in.

The price is naturally one factor you need to consider. But at the same time there are many other conditions one shouldn't lose sight of - suppliers' ability to deliver on time, the continuity of supply, the suppliers' standard of workmanship and their ability to supply to your specification.

SELECTION OF SUBCONTRACTORS

The first thing is - know your subcontractors and suppliers. The Standard requires that you place your order with them on the simple basis of their ability to meet the specification you define.

This demands that you maintain records. I like to see a register of suppliers and sub-contractors that shows me:

- Details of each order placed.
- Their performance in supplying against orders.
- Test records.
- Information on any defects.
- Corrective Action.

Finally, you should be able to demonstrate with tangible evidence that you are carrying out periodic reviews on all your subcontractors. This might include site visits if the purchased items were significant enough.

PURCHASING DATA

When you take delivery of a subcontractor's product they should be required within your processes to supply you with detailed information about the batch of material or the work they have carried out. The extent of the data that you might reasonably expect to receive will vary enormously from item to item. If, for, example we are purchasing an electronic subassembly, then we might also require them to supply a circuit diagram, a technical specification and a summary of any functional testing. On the other hand, the supply of a consignment of resistors may need nothing more than a batch document specifying the tolerance on the notional value within a given temperature range. The important point is that it should be *you* who specifies what data should be included with the purchased product. To this end these requirements should be written in to the order you placed. A final point on this matter; don't demand data that you can't or won't use. All this will do is cloud the real requirements and may result in putting up the costs.

customer

PURCHASER-SUPPLIED PRODUCT

TAKE NOTHING FOR GRANTED

There are occasions when your customer will be supplying parts or even whole sub-assemblies for you to incorporate into the product you are manufacturing on his behalf. This is quite a common practice these days in the electronic manufacturing industry. Take, for example, the etching of printed circuit boards and the mounting of components. The purchaser of the finished board might require some special semiconductors which he will supply to be incorporated into the finished assembly. To maintain your assembly line the purchaser will have provided you with sufficient components to keep your production going.

The Standard requires you to accept certain responsibilities for these parts and can be summarised as follows:

- Keep good records of what items have been provided, including batch numbering, date of arrival, job or contract for which they are destined.

- Carry out some acceptance tests for yourselves. The customer may have carried out tests on the items prior to shipping them to you but this doesn't absolve you from testing them as you would have done had the items had come from a trade source. Consider the embarrassment if you were to miss a key shipping date because components that had been sitting in your stores for 3 months were discovered on the day they were needed to be faulty, or in some other way unsuitable. You could hardly place the blame at his door; you have had 12 weeks to take some action and didn't.

- Are they the right parts? Your customer (who in this case is also your supplier) is just as likely to ship you *all* right-handed doors as any other supplier you deal with. So not only check that they have sent you "good" items, but that they are also the "right" items!

- Know the test status, for example what testing, if any, they have undergone prior to being shipped to you.

- They need to be kept totally segregated from your own stock. If it is at all possible, some form of identification mark or label clearly showing the ownership would also be advisable.

- The items should be stored and handled as befits the nature of the parts. For example, are they sensitive to light or magnetic fields? Do you need to adopt electrostatic protection when handling them? The solution is to know exactly what you are dealing with and get your customer to document how he requires them to be stored and handled.

- Finally, ensure that any loss or damage or otherwise nonconforming items are recorded and reported promptly to your customer.

PRODUCT IDENTIFICATION AND TRACEABILITY

"WHERE APPROPRIATE"

One might, at enormous cost, be able to identify the source of every single item that goes into the manufacture of a product. But in the real world this is neither practical, useful or necessary. The Standard refers to *where appropriate* and leaves it to the good business sense of the manufacturer.

But where it is appropriate it should be possible for a company to trace any product back through the manufacturing process to the specifications and drawings and, moreover, be able to demonstrate that testing, defined as part of the process, has been satisfactorily completed. It is one thing to lay down strict procedures controlling those elements of a product which are created within your company, but quite another when it comes to purchased parts.

There are many ways this can be achieved in a manufacturing process and the optimum method for any particular production line will largely rest on the complexity of the product. One can well imagine a situation where the "manufacturing process" leading to a shipped product consists of no more than that of the assembly of a number of modules which originate from a number of different sources. Some will be minor "off the shelf" standard items such as screws, wire, etc, while other more significant sections will have been bought ready assembled, having been made to your specification by an outside subcontractor. Over and above this, there may be sections of the same product you simply purchase as a standard unit, such as power supplies.

TRACEABILITY

It is only when you start to consider the complexity of some products that you begin to realise the potential for disaster unless considerable care is taken in regard to traceability. You need to be able to confirm by good record keeping and some form of identification that these more significant items continue to be tested in some way to establish their continuing suitability.

One of the first things to do when they arrive at your company premises is get them sample or batch-tested. The next requirement is to establish a flexible method by which you can not only identify their status but also trace their source. Something along the lines of small coloured adhesive labels like the ones illustrated overleaf might well suffice. You could, at a small cost, purchase these in a number of colours.

69

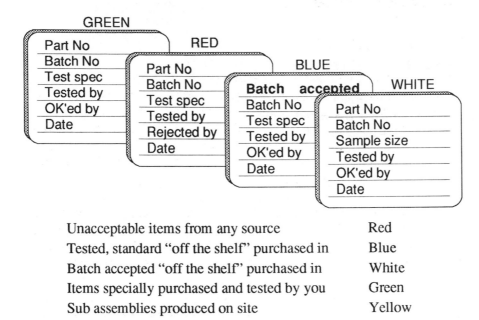

Unacceptable items from any source	Red
Tested, standard "off the shelf" purchased in	Blue
Batch accepted "off the shelf" purchased in	White
Items specially purchased and tested by you	Green
Sub assemblies produced on site	Yellow

Suggested style for labelling of manufacturing items

The manner of testing and the criteria for acceptability is entirely up to you as the manufacturer. The questions to ask yourself are; can I at any stage of the manufacturing process look at a product and trace back where each element of the assembly was obtained? Do I have reasonable confidence, through testing, that it is of acceptable quality?

PROCESS CONTROL

INTRODUCTION

This is a wide ranging clause of the Standard and often the least understood. In its simplest interpretation it requires a company to have a defined and fully documented process to achieve its business objectives. It requires that each step of the production shall be carefully specified and Work Instructions (where applicable) are available. Process Control also includes any production testing carried out and would be expected to include any final acceptance testing of the finished product.

The Standard requires that each step of the production process follows a predetermined plan. It expects that the process, no matter how many steps are involved, has been carefully planned and documented (Procedures) and that adequate check points have been designated throughout the process so as to verify that the end product is of satisfactory quality.

I think I should, in order to make the subject clear, distinguish between a Process, a Project and a Procedure. I have frequently found people confuse Process Management with Project Management and then think of them both as some sort of Procedure. So let us define our terms:

- *A process* is a chain of cross-department activities in an organisation which is frequently repeated in order to achieve some form of output. The phrase "frequently repeated" is significant.
  Examples: 1.   The introduction of a new product.
  2.   The annual review and adjustment of your prices.
  3.   Quality auditing.

- *A project* is a "one-time" exercise put in place to achieve a single designated objective.
  Examples: 1.   Moving the Head Office function to a new location.
  2.   Selecting and launching a new "house style".

- *A procedure* is the defined method by which some element of the company's activity is to be be carried out.
  Examples: 1.   A Procedure to instruct an employee how they are to return faulty supplies back to your manufacturing site.
  2.   How a manager should obtain training for his staff.

71

One key "Process" is the sum of all those sub-activities which constitute the end-to-end production line of your product or the service you are providing your customer. When viewed in this way one begins to realise the importance of the clause; after all this is what the customer is paying good money for.

One of the frequently overlooked aspects of process control is the consequential impact it can have on the range of any subsequent auditing carried out. Be very careful of what you do and don't include within your documented Quality Procedures. It may, for example, be desirable to have the floor swept every morning but if you put that requirement into the documented procedures then anyone auditing the process will expect to find some recorded evidence that it is happening. I've seen some very strange activities built into "the procedures" which either become a millstone round the department's neck, or as is more often the case, gradually become ignored. The question always should be - does it have any bearing on Quality? - and if the answer is "No", then leave it out and deal with it some other way.

PROCESS MANAGEMENT

The more conventional organisational structure of companies in the UK is by departmental disciplines such Design, Engineering, Stores, Marketing and so on. Let me call this "Function Management". The problem with organisation by function is that each can be driven towards independence on the one hand and self-preservation on the other. More enlightened companies have come to realise that it is "the Process" which is perhaps the more important. Yet the process may well depend for its success on significant contributions from many departments.

Let me suggest, to illustrate the point, that we look at what I will call "New Product Process Management". New Era plc have decided to get a slice of the high quality laser printer business, an area they have never ventured into before. Design and Development may need to recruit specialist knowhow. Manufacturing may have no previous experience of laser technology; Stores will need to purchase a whole new range of parts; Purchasing will have to research into who are the likely sub-contractors. And so on, to the point that by the time you have the product in the salesmen's portfolios, everyone will have a finger in it. What is needed is a manager of sufficient seniority and the assigned authority who can organise and drive the Process across all the affected departments. This Process Manager needs to work to "The Grand Plan" and have enough charm (and clout at times) to be able to get each contributing department to commit to their specific objectives.

SERVICE LEVEL AGREEMENTS (SLAs)

SLAs are a very simple but effective method of ensuring that departments work together to attain agreed objectives. Their use as a management tool becomes particularly attractive when one department achievement is dependent on other departments meeting their commitments. If we take the example of of New Era plc and the new laser printer, Marketing wish to offer the customers 98% availability of use. This can only be achieved if the Engineering Department can be sure of training for its staff and spares availability by the Stores. Then Stores are dependent on Manufacturing's ability to switch enough parts from the production line to be available for the Field Service Engineer. The Training Manager will need to have some temporary assignee instructors from the Field Service Engineers if he is to satisfy the training needs that this new product line will generate.

This is an ideal case for the Process Manager to help negotiate interdepartmental SLAs, each one tailored to provide one department with what it requires to meet a contractual obligation it has given to some other department of the company. Somewhere amongst all these interdepartmental demands a reasonably balanced solution can be arrived at and put down in black and white with measurable parameters.

CHANGES IN THE PROCESS

As technology advances or new materials become available, or perhaps as the product basic design is refined against marketplace requirements then changes in the "process" will become inevitable. When this happens, the Standard requires that you incorporate any such changes in a controlled manner. The final authority to approve changes should be restricted to a designated person. There also needs to be evidence that any changes have been subjected to some form of qualifying verification no less vigorous than that applied to the original part of the process being replaced.

The word "process" in the context of BS 5750 isn't restricted simply to the actual creation of the product or service you are in business to supply, but can relate to almost any aspect of your company's Quality System. Let me give you an example. You may have declared in your procedures that all Service Engineers will be formally trained in your own Training School. Let us suppose that you then make a management decision, for whatever reason, that some elements of their training will be carried out by an external organisation. Fine, it may well be that this external training school you have selected is the best in the country, but if I were assessing your company I would be asking to see evidence that this alteration in the Process had been made in a controlled way, that the authority to make the change had been gained, and that some post evaluation had taken place to ensure that it totally met the requirement of your company.

You might be excused for thinking this misdemeanour is against Clause 4.18 of BS 5750 - that of training. No one suggests that the external training course isn't every bit as good as the one which used to be run locally by New Era plc themselves. But what I would ask is, " Who made the decision and has the change been evaluated?" and, most importantly, "Do the documented procedures reflect the change?"

All good companies are dynamic; change is not just unavoidable but desirable if you are to maintain or increase your share of the market. But uncontrolled changes in Process Control quickly breed chaos. The extent of the chaos may not become evident until your customers bring it to your attention, and by then it's often too late.

The cost in real money, customer satisfaction and loyalty, even staff morale, are at risk if you allow changes in the Processes of your business without careful analysis. I would recommend that changes in Processes are treated in many ways like Corrective Actions, the key difference being that the former is fundamentally to alter the process by which something is done, whilst a Corrective Action is to adjust or rectify an established process that is otherwise working fine. There are going to be times when the distinction between Change in Process and Corrective Action is very marginal.

WORK INSTRUCTIONS

Confusion can sometimes be found between Work Instructions and Job Descriptions. The difference is quite simple, in that a Job Description states *what* tasks are the employee's responsibility. A Work Instruction, on the other hand, describes step be step *how* a particular task is to be carried out. In a Quality System both are equally important, since without a Job Description an employee may simply not realise that some vital task is their responsibility. Without a Work Instruction an employee may or may not, for example, know how to correctly "earth" a piece of equipment, and you may not find out until you have seen the coroner's report months later.

Not every single task assigned to an employee requires a Work Instruction. It would be insulting if not ridiculous to write down how every menial task should be executed. Could I suggest a simple test? Ask yourself two questions; Question One, were it to be carried out incorrectly, would it affect

Quality? If the answer is "yes" then you had better have a Work Instruction. Question Two, is it totally self-evident how the task should be carried out even to someone who is new to the company? If the answer in this case is an honest "yes" then I would suggest you probably do not need a Work Instruction.

One last word on Work Instructions - they should be available in the actual place where the task is being carried out. This may seem somewhat self-evident but I know from first hand experience that this, very often, is not the case. "Oh! yes," said a manager to me one day, when I was out with him at a customer site observing an engineer setting up a machine, "They're in my office - I'll show you them when we get back this afternoon".

JOB DESCRIPTIONS

Everyone in an organisation should, without exception, have a Job Description. It should unambiguously define most if not all the following parameters:

- Title of the post.
- Who they report into.
- The staff available.
- Key task responsibilities.
- Make reference to any applicable Work Instructions.
- Define specific performance measurements where applicable.
- Refer to any Service Level Agreements in force.
- Describe any agreed extra duties.
- Specify the minimum training required.

I have come across some very strange pieces of paper posing as Job Descriptions, documents with vague and all-embracing phrases like, "Carry out duties as required" and "Training as defined by the manager". One company I visited did commendably have Job Descriptions for its people, but the only copies available were held by the manager; the staff had never actually seen them, let alone agreed to them.

I have always favoured the notion that employees should be invited, once they have been in the role for a while, to draft out their own Job Descriptions. Not only will they include tasks you were perhaps unaware they performed, but also getting a signed acceptance as to the duties of a post is always easier when the holder of the post wrote them into the document.

It should be evident by means of signatures that both the employee and the manager are in agreement with the contents of any Job Description. Additionally, as with any form of contract, at the end of the day both parties should have a copy of it. Finally, I feel that it is good practice for copies of all Job Descriptions to be held by the Personnel Department, if for no other reason than that they can monitor the range of employee skills required by the many departments of the company and so help place unassigned manpower.

It should be possible to hand such a Job Description to any deputies and be confident that they would have no problem fulfilling the duties of the post.

At the end of this Topic *(pp. 81-83)* you will find I have included an example of both a Work Instruction and Job Description. Their inclusion is simply to show you the level of detail they might be expected to contain. You will notice how the Job Description makes a cross-reference to the Work Instruction.

MEETINGS

I have added the subject of meetings into this general area of Process Control, not because it is given any particular place in the Standard but because it takes up such a lot of management's time and can, if effective, work miracles.

Meetings, I find, fall into two categories, those for simply broadcasting information out to the troops and the second, more open, type, where the discussion of common topics of interest is the aim. I would concede that there is a third class which is a mixture of both.

I am mainly concerned with the second classification, where a group of managers get together to solve the world's problems. These meetings can, in the wrong hands, be about as productive as a wildcat strike and twice as destructive. I speak from bitter experience over many years. It is amazing when one considers the amount of time management devotes to meetings that many seem content to spend the time so unproductively.

Let us start with *Where, When* and *What.*

Unless World War III has broken out and you are responsible for the Defence of the Realm, then I fail to see the justification for the "at the drop of a hat" approach. Three basic requirements should have been provided to all the proposed attendees well in advance:

1.   Precisely *where* the meeting is to be held - building and room.

2.   *When*, a date and time slot. Attendee's should be given a start and finishing time. Fight anyone who tries to impose a vague open ended commitment on your time.

3.   Absolutely paramount, at least a provisional *agenda*. Attendees may need to do some preparation prior to attendance and they can only do this if they know the topics. Maybe they wish to get the views of their own staff. The agenda should also make it clear how an attendee can have a topic of his own added to the agenda. I think it's a sloppy practice to leave this possibility to be covered by "any other business" at the end of the meeting.

ON THE DAY

The best place to hold a meeting of this kind is on neutral ground. A gaggle (four or more managers of equal status) of first-line managers sitting facing a senior manager seated behind his desk, in his office, isn't a meeting - it's an "audience". There is a growing practice these days to furnish meeting rooms with a round table, an excellent idea if you want people to be open and start exchanging thoughts. Having said that, you also want equality around the table with everyone given a chance to make their contribution. Along with that goes the need to maintain balance and focus on the topic under discussion, and let us not forget that the rest of the agenda needs its fair airing. A good Chairperson is worth his or her weight in gold. I also like to see an agenda where each topic has been given a specific time slot, which one can roughly keep to. This also has the advantage that if someone is to attend for just one single topic he or she doesn't have to sit through the whole meeting.

If this is one of a series of meetings, as is often the case, where the "minutes" of the last meeting will be required, you can bet your life that someone will turn up without them. Good chairpersons always seems to have a spare copy at their fingertips.

Who is going to take the "minutes"? In these times when secretaries are becoming a rare breed it is often left to one of the attendees or the Chairperson. I don't like this arrangement since it has two adverse effects. First, it limits one person's contribution since they'll have their head down scribbling away half the time. Second, an attendee with a vested interest might not *exactly* record the conclusion of the meeting.

One possible answer is to get the group to agree that the last person to arrive takes the minutes. I think turning up late for a meeting is frequently nothing more than a discourtesy to everyone else who arranged their affairs so that the meeting could start on time, so this extra duty many have an improving side-effect.

The style of the "minutes" of the meeting is worth a few words. For a start, if you come up with a good format, why not make it standard across the company? The difficulty is normally one of continuity, as unresolved items pass on from one meeting to the next until they can be finally closed. Another sin is either that there are so many words that nobody takes the trouble to read them, or so few words that the minutes, when read a couple of days later, are so cryptic as to have no meaning.

You will notice I refered in the last paragraph to " ...the minutes, when read a couple of days later". How often have you arrived at one meeting and for the first time been handed a copy of the minutes of the previous one? Not really good enough, I would say, particularly if there were action points assigned to you.

Once in a while I feel it's a worthwhile practice to get an independent opinion as to the quality of the meetings you hold. Consider getting a manager from another group to act as a "fly on the wall". If you do this, then do be careful to explain the purpose to the attendees and request their permission. One other valuable way to determine if your meetings are productive and a pleasure to attend - do a survey of the attendees from time to time.

A few words about the other form of meeting, where it is intended to give out essential business information, frequently to a large audience. There are bound to be a few who, for quite acceptable reasons, are unable to attend - sickness, holidays, away on training, etc. How can you, at some later date be sure that everyone has had the benefit of the new information? A good practice is to pass around a listing of all the people you would like to have been there and let the attendees sign the sheet. You are then better able to administer any follow-up.

CONCLUDING COMMENT

I started out this discussion on Clause 4.9 of the Standard by stating that it was wide ranging, and on this statement I rest my case. As you are now able to see, Process, in the terms of the Standard, can be anything at all related to the actual product/services your company supplies to the customers. In fact, I would go a step further and say that if you have documented that a thing will happen, then that has become part of your Process and therefore there must be evidence that it is under control.

Sample of a Job Description:

Engineering Job Description 27   Issue 4
Customer Service Supervisor   Page 1+

JOB TITLE   Customer Service Supervisor

REPORTING TO   Customer Services Manager

REPORTING STAFF   4 Customer Service Coordinators

KEY TASK RESPONSIBILITIES

- The general daily supervision of the Customer Service Facility.

- Produce a weekly staffing rota to ensure adequate staffing throughout normal business hours.

- Escalate to the appropriate Field Engineering Manager any Service Request which is in jeopardy of exceeding the agreed response time.

- Produce a daily back-up of the Customer Service database at the close of business each day (refer to Work Instruction E3001).

- Ensure that POWER DOWN procedures are well understood by the staff and conduct at least one unannounced "live" test a year.

- Gather new and updated information on engineers, customers and equipment. Input the database once a week with any new and confirmed information.

- Monitor "Time to answer the telephone" by the coordinators and produce weekly statistics of your findings for management.

- Conduct monthly Quality of Work checks on each member of your staff.

ADDITIONAL ASSIGNED SPECIAL DUTIES

- Prepare and run two "Customer Days" a year to illustrate to our customers the working of the Customer Service Facility.
  The invited group of customers per visit must not exceed 12 (target date for first session 1/11/92).

81

> ### *Engineering Job Description 27*   Issue 4
> ### *Customer Service Supervisor*   Page 2 -

● Develop a method to ascertain the level of Customer Satisfaction the service the department provides (target date 1/1/92).

PERFORMANCE MEASUREMENTS

● "Time to Answer the telephone" should not exceed 25 seconds.

TRAINING FOR ROLE

● Dealing with customers   2-day course (booked for Nov 91)
● Supervisor skills   3-day course (completed)

Signed as agreed..................   Line Manager................

Date.............   Date ....

Sample of a Work Instruction:

Engineering Work Instruction 31   Issue 3

Database daily back-up   Page 1 -

ENGINEERING CUSTOMER DATABASE BACK-UP

The database holding all our current customer information, such as their addresses, the equipment they have installed, and any outstanding maintenance service they require, is held on a 60-million character storage device (hard-disk) in the IBM Personal Computer. This database also holds vital additional information regarding the engineers and the scope of their training. If, due to a malfunction, this information were lost or corrupted it would seriously impact the service to the customers. For this reason it is imperative that we make daily "copies" of the data so we could recover the situation. This process is known as *Back-up*. The Back-up process is to be carried out by the Supervisor at the end of each working day.

PROCESS

1.   At the end of each working day take, from the Fire Safe in the manager's office, the set of disks marked with the current day (e.g. Friday).

2.   Place the first disk of the set into the "A" drive and close down the flap.

3.   Ensure that the PC screen is displaying the correct date and time. If incorrect then adjust.

4.   From the Master Menu screen, select the option BACK-UP.

5.   Follow the instructions displayed on the screen.

6.   At the end of the process the screen will again display the Master Menu. At this stage remove the final disk from the "A" drive and return the full set of disks to the Fire Safe.

7.   Enter details of your actions in the Daily Duty Log, e.g. BACK-UP TAKEN 19:37 hrs 30/8/91 (Friday) P.K.Thompson

Note: If you encounter any difficulties in carrying out this Work Instruction then contact the Technical Support Team for assistance.

INSPECTION AND TESTING

INTRODUCTION

The intention of this clause is to ensure that basically four things are taken care of:

1.   That incoming materials - spares, sub-assemblies etc, are of known good quality.

2.   That testing and inspection is an inherent part of the manufacture or installation.

3.   That the finished product is subjected to final inspection and testing before it is supplied to the customer.

4.   That you keep documented evidence that the above three factors have been addressed.

Any materials you purchase, whether they are to be included in the manufacturing process of your product, or as spares to be used in a repair service, must meet the standards of acceptability your company specify. Evidence should also be available to confirm that all the inspections and tests required to be conducted by your suppliers have been carried out.

PHASES OF INSPECTION AND TESTING

So let us examine these phases during which attention to Inspection and Testing needs to be considered.

As goods are received
Here you can generally only verify two things; first, that the item is what was ordered, for example, that you have received a MDX1220 Power Unit rated at 12v 20A and not a MDX1205 which supplies only a quarter of the required power; second, that it visually appears to be of satisfactory manufacture. In the case of more expensive or critical items you would be well advised to send the unit to some testing department before accepting it into stock.

During the process of assembly
Generally the amount of testing which can be done during the assembly stage is very limited. If the item is critical and difficult to replace once the

85

assembled unit is completed, then have the component tested while it is still in held stock. But "inspection" is often easier during assembly, as also are corrections. Later on when the total product is finished it may be difficult to even see a unit, much less inspect it.

On completion of the total product
I am only happy when there are clearly documented inspection and test specifications for assembled units. The inspection and testing should, I feel, be carried out by people quite independent from those involved in the manufacture. Have a look at the sample Manufacturing Procedure 23 (Product Testing) I have provided in Part 3 *(p. 211)*

TESTING OF DELIVERED ITEMS

This Standard doesn't specify what nature of testing you should carry out, or the sample rate. These are matters for you to determine. Let us imagine you were purchasing a DC power unit to install within a burglar alarm system your company were manufacturing. You will most probably have specified in considerable detail the parameters and characteristics you require of the unit:

- Output voltage.
- Stability under specific load conditions.
- Permitted AC ripple.
- Heat dissipation.
- Electromagnetic radiation.

There may be other parameters you know to be critical to the purpose the unit will serve in your product. The question this clause of the Standard asks is, how do you ensure that the unit meets your stringent requirements?

You may well choose to send a sample of each delivery to your own testing department and, if that passes your full specification, then only sample check the output voltage of, say, a 5% sample. Other less critical items may require nothing more than a visual inspection. The important points to bear in mind are:

1. The range and detail of testing should be related to the importance of the item's use.

2. You really only need to test those characteristics of the component which directly affect performance against specification. Generally speaking, the tighter the specifications the higher the cost, so don't put

your costs up by demanding that the supplier provide you with a product to a specification beyond that which you really need. You may perhaps choose to include the cosmetic appearance of your finished product in the range of output checks, particularly if it is for the domestic consumer market.

3. Keep good records of the tests you do and be able to identify those parts which were tested and to what level of test they were subjected. The records should be able to identify the units, state the pass/fail status and illustrate what Corrective Action was taken when a unit failed.

4. Review your supplier's performance at meaningful intervals to determine if you can reduce the level of testing or, more importantly, if you need to tighten up the specification. You may take the attitude that it is your supplier's responsibility to provide you with good items conforming to your specification, in which case you may be justified in reducing the extent of the testing you need to carry out. This could, of course, cut your overall costs, but you had better be sure of your ground before taking this step.

5. You should make certain that your supplier has only very limited authority to modify the specification. If he has to change the assembly in any way then it should be a requirement of his contract with your company that he informs you of what changes he proposes to make, and for what reasons. You may also need to modify your own acceptance testing until you are satisfied with any agreed modifications.

POST-PRODUCTION TESTING

such as ?

There may be times when a purchased item for inclusion into your company's final product can't be fully tested until the product has passed well down the production process. When this happens there has to be some distinctive method by which you can identify these, as yet, unapproved items.

TEST STATUS SHEET

I have included a form called a Test Status Sheet in Part 3 *(p.200)*. You might find this a useful base document to track a product manufacture or even the installation process of a system. The form could be adapted to almost any product or service, for that matter. The user would need to define (by means of Work Instructions) the various tests (or inspections) which were required to be carried out during the assembly. I have left space for up to 10 of these specific tests; you would just blank out those you didn't require. The form then provides an area where details of the final tests can be noted. The form then, at the end of all the stages of manufacture, provides a single sheet record of:

- Product type details and customer information.
- What tests have been carried out and by whom.
- Signed evidence that it was deemed fit for shipment to the customer.

UNTESTED ITEMS

This is going to be the exception rather than the rule, but there are times when purchased items will have to be pressed directly into service. We don't have total control over the suppliers and so this is going to happen occasionally. Under such circumstances, BS 5750 requires you to record their use and be able to identify any affected units. This is clearly in case you find a problem and you need to take some form of retroactive action to solve it.

STOCK HOLDING AREAS

There should be a number of quite distinctive and clearly marked sections in any stock holding area:

Goods in.	Delivery holding area.
Goods out.	Finished product destined for your customer.
Quarantine.	Parts which are suspect and shouldn't be issued.
Nonconforming.	Parts which have failed acceptability.
Main Section.	With good parts tested and found acceptable and under proper stock control.
Customer-owned.	Parts supplied by specific customers for inclusion in equipment they are having built by you or for service activity on their equipment.

RECORDS

Finally, since so much effort has gone into the inspection and testing of materials, purchased sub-assemblies, components, the construction of the object and then the testing of the finished product, you need to have a system of record keeping that will enable you to review your findings.

INSPECTION, MEASURING AND TEST EQUIPMENT

MAYBE YOU HAVE TOO MUCH

The Standard goes to great lengths in relation to this particular clause and so I have likewise endeavoured to give you as much guidance as I can on the subject. Most of the cases I have come across where a company is having trouble keeping track of its test equipment happens because it simply has too much for its needs. Before plunging headlong into an expensive and administratively difficult scheme for calibration, ask yourself, "What do we need?" rather than, "What do we have?" Here are a few simple steps that could save your company a lot of money and make life simpler:

1. Call in any equipment that isn't actually required and either scrap, sell or at least for the moment put it in quarantine until you decide on its future.

2. If an instrument is being used for nothing more elaborate than checking fuses or finding out if a voltage is present or not, then why have it calibrated at all? All you need to do is affix a clear label on it which declares it to be "Uncalibrated - indication only".

3. If your engineers only need to use "calibrated" test equipment once or twice a year then it may be more practical to hold such items in the local office (under controlled conditions). In this way, what are frequently expensive, delicate devices don't spend 11 months of the year bouncing about in the boot of a car.

4. After applying the three ideas suggested above, consider the quantity of devices left which need annual calibration. There may be enough to warrant you verifying the accuracy yourselves. This can be achieved by checking them against a known reference standard which is itself traceable back to a National Standard.

You should now be able to draw up an inventory of test equipment which falls within the calibration process. An easy problem to resolve is identification of test devices. The serial numbers given by the manufacturers of the devices tend to be variable in their format and always lengthy. I would advise you to give every instrument within your system a unique, short serial number of your own and label the devices with that identity. All you need to do then is keep one central list in the local documentation which could be used to

match the two numbers. What I have in mind is M01, M02, etc. for meters
and S01, S02, and so on for oscilloscopes. The list would look something
like:

Local No	Full description
M01	Fluke digital MTR Ser No345290/a
M02	AVO Analog Ser No 47300B
S01	Techtronic Model 5 Ser No 03451/S

INTEGRITY

You are required to make sure that once a piece of testing equipment has been
calibrated or verified then the instrument is in some way sealed against
anyone tampering with it. Meters coming back from a testing laboratory
usually have three indicators; a separate test certificate giving any indication
deviations; a label on the device stating the dates of most recent calibration
and possibly the date it will next need to be verified; finally, there must be
some tamper-proof seal to the case or over any adjustment screws which are
accessible from outside the case.

When an instrument has been calibrated, or verified, the testing house may
draw your attention to the fact that it was outside the acceptable range of
tolerance when it was sent to them. Make sure that any procedure you draft
to cover test equipment gives clear advice as to what should be done in such
a situation. The reasoning is evident but frequently overlooked. It could well
be that every thermostat on your production line has been set wrongly
because a reference thermometer was incorrect or electronic equipment is
running in customer's premises with voltages set well below the
manufacturer's specification. The answer is clearly, at minimum, to review
the use of the equipment prior to it being sent away and re-evaluating any
measurements if you feel necessary.

I have found that companies establish the frequency of re-calibration when
they first introduce a device into the system and never review the periodicity.
I think procedures should specify in some way that instruments which, over
a series of re-calibration checks have been seen to hold their setting could be
given a longer period between checks. Why waste money? On the other hand

any equipment seen to drift away from its designed setting should have the interval between checks decreased; in fact, it may be advisable and more economic to scrap the device altogether.

CORRECT FOR THE TASK

You need to review the use an instrument is put to before you can be certain of its acceptability, even when it is within correct calibration. For example, if a potentiometer has to be set to a precise value of within 1% then there is little use measuring it with a meter that can only indicate resistance within 10%.

In summary:

- Know what you need.
- Keep on eye on calibration.
- Keep good records.
- Apply good housekeeping.

I have included a form in Part 3 (E1101, *p.187*) which might prove useful to you.

INSPECTION AND TEST STATUS

OVERVIEW

As a product passes through the various stages of production (or installation) it has to be possible to establish exactly what tests have been carried out. Clause 4.10 of the Standard has gone to great lengths as to the amount of testing you may have to carry out from the early stage of receiving material right through to the finished deliverable product. The details of these tests has to be clearly defined, for example how they are to be carried out and under what environmental conditions.

Now it remains for you to find some way by which you can signify that the article has passed all these specified inspections and tests. Having declared what constitutes a "pass", it's now necessary for you to identify the fact. The *final* inspection or test should include the requirement to look for confirmation that these various "in-production" checks, tests, inspections, call them what you will, have been satisfactorily completed.

The objective is that at the end of the production line or the completion of an installation it has to be possible to demonstrate that all the individual specified tests and inspections *were* conducted, by *whom*, and most importantly were found to be *satisfactory*.

LABELLING

How you record the information can vary enormously, ranging from identification tags and labels, to test sheets or routing cards. There are many ways of doing this and you need to come up with a scheme which suits your company and your product. You may be able to adapt the labels I described under the topic of Product Identification - (see Part 1 Topic 4.8)

AUTHORISATION

There are a couple of important extra requirements you need to meet and they concern "authorisation". You need to define somewhere, in your documentation, who on your staff is qualified to declare that a test has been passed. Finally the marking should make it possible to trace back who actually gave that particular test the "thumbs up". As you can, see the whole thing is to do with *tracebility*.

TEST PARAMETERS

It may not, in some situations, be acceptable to state a simple pass or fail criteria. Specific results may have to be defined in terms of physical parameters (e.g. voltage, temperature, etc.). All these inspections and tests will need detailed specifications in the appropriate documentation (see Topic 4.10) and the results recorded.

SUMMARY

1.   Define and document what tests are to be carried out.
2.   Define what constitutes an acceptable item.
3.   List who is authorised to do the tests.
4.   Carry out the tests and identify who did them.
5.   Place the "test status" on the item itself if at all possible.
6.   Reject those which fail the test criteria.
7.   Keep detailed records of fail/pass to form useful statistics.
8.   Review the failures for possible corrective action.

CONTROL OF NONCONFORMING PRODUCT

NO-ONE IS PERFECT

May I start out by reminding you of Murphy's Law? - *"If a thing can go wrong, it will go wrong"*.

The Standard accepts that we don't live in a perfect world and no matter how tight your control systems may be, some things are going to go wrong, for whatever reason. What is important is that once you have established that a product, a part, or whatever is unsatisfactory in some way, and it fails your own level of acceptability, then there are procedures to deal with the situation. Good record keeping in this area is absolutely vital.

In the case of physical items such as parts, assemblies or completed product *segregation* is definitely the key word. Under no circumstances should such items be allowed to become inadvertently mixed in with good items. The other measure you should have in place is to identify clearly any such items by whatever method best suits your needs, labels, tie-on tags, etc. It has to be possible, either from the label or some attached report, to know exactly what has been discovered wrong. The conditions of the Standard, if they have been adhered to, should enable you trace the production of the item and investigate what went wrong. This should automatically open a path to the subsequent Corrective Action you need to take to avoid repetition.

Nonconforming to customer request.

I can't resist the opportunity to relate the story (probably apocryphal) about the shipment of transistors received by a UK manufacturer from a Far East supplier. When the box containing the ordered 1000 items was opened they discovered an additional 22 transistors in a separate plastic bag labelled "DEFECTIVE". When asked to explain, the agent of the supplier said that the order had puzzled the supplier as *their* Quality Control didn't permit the shipment of faulty items but in order to satisfy the terms of the order, and he quoted the purchase document sent to the Far East - "Defective items to be limited to 5% of the shipment" - the bag was their response in order to meet their contractual obligation.

*done at 11 am &
at 2 pm at Nissan Mfg, UK
during
gathering
of all
line leaders*

It is essential that you incorporate within the system some formal review of nonconforming products and materials. A company can learn a lot about its processes and their weaknesses by making a detailed examination of its failures. If I were running such a review it would have the following agenda in mind:

- Statistical performance.
- The cost of failure.
- Corrective Actions.
- Examine the key failing production areas.
- Changes to Procedures and processes.
- Disposal of nonconforming items.
- Customer Contractual issues.

Finally, and equally important, if you have to rework any items, don't overlook the fact that they must be subjected to all the production tests and inspections as they go round the loop again.

CORRECTIVE ACTION

INTRODUCTION

Without a well defined and effective Corrective Action process the rest of the Quality System you put in place ends up being nothing more than cosmetic. If you consider the aim of a Quality System is to bring your company closer and ever closer to that elusive state of perfection, then Corrective Action has a key role to play in getting you there. The perfect company has yet to be developed; there are a lot of good ones about and even a few excellent ones, but I have yet to see a perfect company. Corrective Action, if properly applied, will get you one step nearer that goal.

GETTING THINGS PUT RIGHT

The Corrective Action (CA) process can, and I feel should, be standardised right across a company and should be applied as a working practice in every department. A well designed process of CA can fix most problems from the staff canteen food to ensuring your suppliers send you only the highest quality materials.

CA is often thought of as a consequence of finding something wrong during an audit and so calling for someone to put something right. But why stop at Quality Audits, why not give everyone in the company the opportunity to bring nonconformities to the notice of somebody who is in a position to do something about it? But for the moment we will stay within the brief of BS 5750. All the audits, reviews and reappraisals are worthless unless they are followed up by a closely monitored corrective action process. The mechanism is so simple one wonders why so many people have such problems.

Let's look at the steps in the most simple model we can devise.

We take an intelligent look at some function for which we have no direct responsibility; in a word we are independent. We try to understand what objective the function has. We also must consider the route to be taken to achieve that objective.

The next step would be to establish if the practice being followed was in any way a deviation from that documented and prescribed. We can then go on to ask the question, was the objective reached?

97

Now we are in a position to define, and hopefully get agreement to, an appropriate Corrective Action plan. Remember there are basically six steps to any good Corrective Action:

1.   You only need to specify what is wrong, not how to solve it.
2.   Establish who is the problem OWNER since he is the right person to fix it.
3.   Get the agreement of the OWNER that what you are saying about his piece of the action has been accurately described.
4.   Get them to agree to a date by which it will be put right.
5.   Monitor to ensure it happens as agreed.
6.   Finally, go back some time later and confirm that it has stayed fixed.

Be alert to those who would simply patch over a problem; the key objective of Corrective Action is to remedy the problem permanently, not to get round it by means of some sort of a temporary fix. Not that I think there is anything wrong with a temporary fix (see Concession on Page 99) if, for good reasons, that happens to be the preferred option at the time.

The usual reasons for procedures not being followed is that they are either inappropriate, out of date or perhaps simply don't work. In such situations the best thing to do is to raise a Corrective Action and get the procedure changed. .

The key to a successful CA process has to be the disciplines within the organisation, and this appears to work best when the control and monitoring is entrusted to an independent office, such as the Quality Department.

I have included a form Q1403 *(p. 195)* which, if not immediately applicable to your needs, could with very little effort be adapted. As you can see it requires the person requesting the CA to fully define the problem as they see it. It should be borne in mind that CA is not the same as either the company Suggestion Scheme or a Discrepancy uncovered during an Quality Audit, in that CA is primarily designed to either improve or put right something which isn't working as originally intended. Furthermore it should be restricted to those elements of the company which directly affect the Quality processes in place.

Let us look at a practical, but not atypical, case of CA and see how to should work:

1.   It has been discovered by a Storeman that an externally purchased circuit board is being packed only in "bubble foil". The Procedures for such stock makes it quite clear that these items should additionally be supplied totally enclosed in an antistatic bag.

2.   The storeman has raised a Corrective Action Request Form, giving as much information as he can, details such as manufacturer, supplier, item identification such as model number, batch number, quantity involved, date of delivery and so on. The form is then sent to the Quality Dept.

3.   The storekeeper places the affected items in quarantine pending a decision.

4.   The Quality Department recognise that this is a problem which could hold up production and affect outstanding customer orders. They log the problem and pass the information quickly on to Purchasing.

5.   Purchasing arrange for the quarantined items to be replaced urgently by the suppliers. They also instruct the Storeman to box up, label and return the items to the supplier.

6   The Quality Department make a note to check with stores in say a month or two to ensure that the problem was permanently fixed.

Because there was an easy-to-use process available, the Storeman had no worry about raising the matter. He knew he couldn't fix the problem but the process didn't require him to. All he had to do was write down a few words on one sheet of paper and things started to happen. Very often problems are swept to one side, only to reappear later as probable disasters, just because trying to find the right person to deal with them (i.e. the problem owner) is too complicated.

CONCESSIONS

There will be times when certain procedures and work instructions have to be temporarily changed or even suspended; for example, when a new manager takes over a department or during a reorganisation. Any such suspension of agreed procedures must be very carefully controlled and have specific time restraints set on it. It mustn't be allowed to be an excuse to let the Quality System fall into disrepair. I believe the key to an effective

Concession Procedure is to entrust it to the Quality Department. Only they would be permitted to allow a concession and define the nature and terms.

Example of a Concession

Let us imagine a simple example of a Concession to see how it might work. Have a look at the Concession form (Q 1405 *p.197*) to follow the activity.

The Stores have a Work Instruction which requires that all electronic circuit boards be packed first in a sealed electrostatic bag. This is then enclosed in a cardboard and foam rubber envelope. Finally this assembly should be packed for shipment to the user in a cardboard box filled with expanded plastic chips. The problem is a simple one - Stores are frequently running out of these plastic packing chips and want to be able to use plastic bubble sheeting as an alternative packing material.

There may be very good technical reasons why the chips are used instead of bubble plastic, which the Stores Manager may not be aware of. It may, on the other hand, be simply a question of cost. So the Stores should fill in a Concession form with the details of the requirement and pass the request to the Quality Department so they can go find out on their behalf. The Engineering Design department are responsible for the circuit board in question and they are the best people to give a considered technical opinion.

Let us suppose that Engineering Design confirm that there will be no detrimental side-effects to the components. The Purchasing Department are also consulted and they confirm that the cost differential of "bubble" versus "chips" is insignificant. The Quality Department are now in a position to issue a Concession to the Stores. This should be for a reasonable period of time to allow the stores to renew the supply of "chips". They may also want to find a secondary source.

Armed with the information they now have, the Quality Department could take the matter a step further and encourage the "owner" to change the documented procedure and describe the acceptability of "bubble" as well as "chips" for packing printed circuit boards. This would greatly reduce the possibility of the problem arising again.

The whole idea of a Concession Procedure is to ensure that temporary problems get prompt but carefully considered temporary solutions. Frequently, as was shown in the simple example we have just seen of "bubble versus chips", ways are discovered to improve the documented procedures to everyone's satisfaction. Without a Concession Procedure, resourceful employees will generally find makeshift and not always suitable answers, just so they can get on with the job in hand.

CUSTOMER COMPLAINTS

I think we all know the name of one major High Street retail outlet which has capitalised on customer complaints by turning them around to become an opportunity to impress the complainer. Even if we are not dealing with the High Street shopper and exchanging the faulty item is not always what our complaining customer requires, we could, nevertheless, learn much from the positive attitude adopted by them since it has much to commend it.

I've been asked very often "What should we class as a complaint?" This isn't a naive question by any means; it is sometimes difficult to define the border between complaint and enquiry. For example, would you class a phone call along these lines as a complaint: "We were told your engineer would be here before lunch and here it is, mid-afternoon, and no sign of him !" I would see this more as an enquiry as to where the elusive engineer has got to and when can we really expect to see him. Nothing is going to be gained by putting this phone call through some sort of administration process. The solution in this case is firstly a sympathetic hearing, a few apologetic words, and some positive reaction.

Some companies take the attitude that only a complaint by letter constitutes a recordable complaint. I don't take this view myself, since I have seen many situations where the seriousness of a complaint and the need of instant action has dictated that the complaint had to be made quickly by the customer. For example, a phone call from a customer: "We only had one of our terminals out of action when we called for a Service Engineer, and now your engineer has worked on the problem all three of them are off the air !" I would judge this to be a serious, recordable complaint. The customer isn't going to forget this incident and would expect us to investigate the circumstances.

One of the advantages of having a formal process to deal with complaints is that employees are more ready to accept them on behalf of the company. It is understandable why some employees, when talking to a disgruntled customer on the phone, avoid giving their name. They fear getting saddled with a problem which they can't resolve because they don't know who can fix it, and even if they did, they haven't the authority to push the matter through. A formal system gets over all these difficulties.

On the next page you will find a very simple flow chart of a suitable process to complement the Q1402 form, Customer Complaint Record. supplied in Part 3 *(p.194)* of this manual.

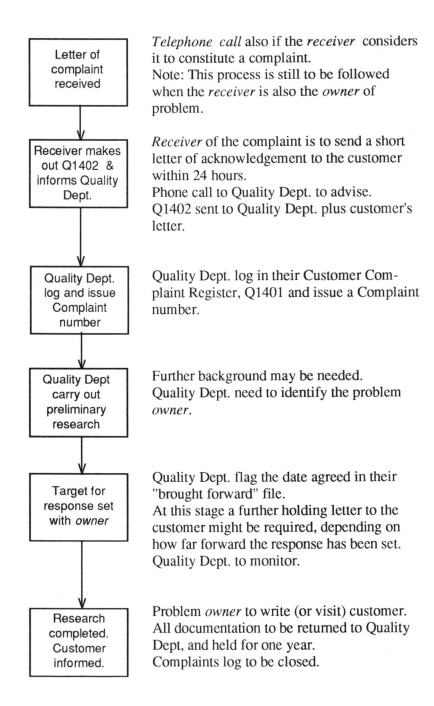

Letter of complaint received	*Telephone call* also if the *receiver* considers it to constitute a complaint. Note: This process is still to be followed when the *receiver* is also the *owner* of problem.
Receiver makes out Q1402 & informs Quality Dept.	*Receiver* of the complaint is to send a short letter of acknowledgement to the customer within 24 hours. Phone call to Quality Dept. to advise. Q1402 sent to Quality Dept. plus customer's letter.
Quality Dept. log and issue Complaint number	Quality Dept. log in their Customer Complaint Register, Q1401 and issue a Complaint number.
Quality Dept carry out preliminary research	Further background may be needed. Quality Dept. need to identify the problem *owner*.
Target for response set with *owner*	Quality Dept. flag the date agreed in their "brought forward" file. At this stage a further holding letter to the customer might be required, depending on how far forward the response has been set. Quality Dept. to monitor.
Research completed. Customer informed.	Problem *owner* to write (or visit) customer. All documentation to be returned to Quality Dept, and held for one year. Complaints log to be closed.

Customer Complaints Process

ZERO DEFECT

There was a time when producing defective items was almost considered a natural consequence of any production line or repetitive manufacturing operation. The answer was, of course, to always make the odd 10% more than was needed so you could make up the shortfall on the order. Manufacturing things so you can scrap them is an astonishing concept when you think about it. But that's the way it was done, and as long as you didn't ship these rejects out to the customer it was seen as a perfectly acceptable way to conduct business. Scrap must have been a significant element in the economics of industry of the UK for many years and it may, for all I know, still be happening in some of our less enlightened companies.

The Japanese developed quite a different approach towards defects. They refused to accept defects as an inevitable part of manufacturing and started to investigate the cause of the failures. From this evolved the "Zero Defect" philosophy and, as they say, the rest is history. In case my reader is not aware of the technique it is worth a short explanation.

At the end of a production line a meaningful number of rejected products are examined so they can be categorised by defect. Let us take some fairly simple product; a hair-dryer, to illustrate the process as carried out by a manufacturer. Here in Fig. 1 is a bar chart of the results obtained as percentage of the total sample of 243 defective hair-dryers:

Rank	Cause	%	Qty
1	Fan & speed control	41	99
2	Heater and its control	26	61
3	Case and cosmetic	19	44
4	Cable and plug	12	29
5	Other	4	10

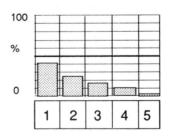

Fig 1

Next were examined the 99 fan and speed control rejects to see what they revealed, since they were the largest single group of rejects. The analysis of these 99 rejected fans showed that well over half were due to poor soldering. The statistical results are shown in Fig. 2.

Rank	Cause	Qty
1	Wiring and solder	58
2	Loose fan	22
3	Motor failure	12
4	Fixture of motor	5
5	Noisy	2

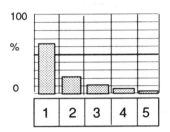

Fig 2

There were 4 soldering stations on the production line and it was found that the 27 rejects came from one employee. It was quickly discovered that this particular person's soldering iron was faulty and never reached the correct temperature. The manager, when told, took a number of actions:

1.   Replaced the defective soldering iron.
2.   Purchased a soldering iron thermometer.
3.   Issued a Work Instruction to the effect that all operatives using soldering irons were to check that the tip temperature reached was within an acceptance temperature range each morning before any work commenced.
4.   Made arrangements for the thermometer reading to be verified at 6-monthly intervals, as recommended by its manufacturer.

The inclination is to try to reduce the failure of the fan assembly further by having an investigation into Cause 2, the loose fan. But no, go back to square one as it were, and review all the defects (less the category you have just fixed), recalculate, and see what it tells you.

Rank	Cause	%	Qty
1	Heater and its control	33	61
2	Case and cosmetic	24	44
3	Fan & speed control	22	41
4	Cable and plug	15	29
5	Other	6	10

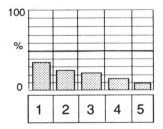

Fig 3

As you can see in Fig.3, there is now more to be gained by investigating the heater and its control, since the fan has dropped down to third place.

Clearly, if it were obvious from an examination of the fan assembly that one could see a simple fix to prevent the fans from coming loose, then one might put that right at the same time. But don't waste too much time on the fan assembly at this stage. Better to spend time finding out what was wrong with those 61 heater assemblies: that also may be something which could be rectified as quickly as was the soldering on the fan.

And so the process goes on, returning to the initial batch to re-evaluate what to investigate and solve next, until the reject samples can tell you no more. The next stage is to take another batch of rejects (of about the same sample size or larger) from the production line, once all the improvements have been made. If there is any justice in the world you are going to have to wait a little longer, since you are not manufacturing as many defective hair-dryers as you used to do.

You could go round and round this loop:

removing the causes of defects in the production line until you reach the state of "Zero Defects", but the question of economics begins to enter the frame. There will be two situations which will influence the aim of "Zero Defects". First, what should be done, if anything, about the purely random defects? They should be few in number and hopefully, small as a percentage of your output. The second situation requires very careful judgement. What if the cost of putting something right greatly outweighs the benefits gained by fixing it? In these situations, every case would need to be assessed in terms of its effect on sales, the public's image of the product, and most importantly, safety.

So "Zero Defect" is a fine policy to adopt, but management judgement needs to come into it at some stage.

HANDLING, STORAGE, PACKAGING AND DELIVERY

INTRODUCTION

The first thing to you should do is go and see how materials and parts are dealt with today. Review the process from end to end and bear in mind there are at least two paths to be considered, one as materials arrive and the second as finished products make their way out to the customer.

HANDLING

Handling is not just a question of how items are physically lifted and put down. In these days of microelectronics a circuit board can be seriously damaged by simply touching the circuit components. This comes from the discharging of a high static potential charge which builds up in the human operative as they go about their normal duties. Ambient conditions such as a dry atmosphere, combined with man-made fibres in clothing and carpeting, can amplify the situation. Most of us have felt the tingle and sometimes seen the blue flash which accompanies such a discharge. These are very high voltages and frequently high current; the only reason they seem no more than an uncomfortable small jolt to the unfortunate human is because the discharge is extremely short in duration, millionths of a second. But that's quite long enough to totally destroy a modern micro-chip semi-conductor. What can be even worse is when such a discharge only partly burns out a circuit path and the component is put into service only to fail at some crucial time weeks or months later.

However, all this can be avoided by good electrostatic discharge (ESD) practice. The solution is very simple and should be employed in any area of a company where staff have a need to handle modern circuit components. All that is required is to bring the handler and the component to the same potential while restricting to a minimum the flow of current (it's the current that does the damage). You will find a number of electronic supply outlets who are able to provide the various, quite low cost, components you will need along with instructions for use. These items include conductive mats, special connecting cords and wrist-straps. You can even get wrist-straps now that double as inexpensive wrist-watches which encourages people to wear them. You should also invest in a simple tester to validate that the components are functioning correctly. I have been frequently been asked - "How do I know when I should be wearing my strap? The answer is - "any time you are not in bed or the bath!"

Just one final point regarding ESD; having put protection in place you will need to demonstrate that some form of testing of the "protection facility" is being carried out at sensible intervals. There are some simple, inexpensive, battery-driven devices available for this purpose on the market.

Returning to the more general aspects of handling, one should pay attention to the manner of handling larger physical units such that they are not a risk to the people around them, but also that they are not likely to suffer damage when being handled. It should be borne in mind that as items are moved (sometimes across the world) not everyone called upon to move your three-ton electronic assembly will know which way is "up" or where you can and can't put lifting chains. Properly marking the outside of the package has got to be cheaper and less hassle than replacing the unit because of damage in transit.

STORAGE

There are usually a number of fragmented stores within a main stock-holding department, be it a warehouse or a small sub-stores. You need to have all these stock-holding sections of your company clearly defined and well segregated areas for both goods inwards and outwards, and within these areas there should be positive segregation of the various categories of materials that may be held. You should, during your reviews, be looking to see what has been done to accommodate all these different class of material:

- Returns for repair.
- Finished repairs awaiting return to the owner.
- Materials owned by customers.
- Special materials purchased against a specific job.
- Sensitive, dangerous and inflammable material.
- Newly-arrived material not yet within the system.
- Nonconforming materials.
- Scrap awaiting disposal.

A great deal of expense and consequential problems can be incurred by the way you deal with stored parts. Loss and breakage are only the visible elements; add to this the discreet damage, customer dissatisfaction and staff demoralisation.

SHELF LIFE and VERIFICATION

"First in, first out" (FIFO) of stored items is an excellent practice but needs keen discipline to ensure it happens. It also demands that you date-stamp or batch-mark every item put on the shelf. Furthermore, the only way to encourage the "pulling" of items in the correct chronological sequence is in the way you stack them. No-one is going to reach to the back of a shelf trying to find the oldest part.

You will also need to give special attention to "shelf life" items. Remember, for example, that many electronic circuit boards these days carry "on-board" batteries. I feel the best way to deal with "on-board" batteries is to fix a prominent label on the outside of the packing box showing the date by which the battery must be replaced.

STOCK CHECKING

My advice would be, don't count low cost parts such as fuses or bulbs or any of those day-to-day consumables peculiar to your business; the exercise will cost more to implement than it will ever save. Just ensure you have enough to satisfy demand. Concentrate on getting and keeping control of the material which costs "real" money or has a long replacement time.

There are many simple methods by which a Stock Centre can keep an eye on inventory levels. Count the quantity left after every withdrawal of an item. Alternatively, do a "cyclic check" each week so that the whole stores holding has been checked, section by section, over a full or half year cycle. These almost effortless yet efficient and regular checks will make the annual full stock checking less of an ordeal.

STOCK CONTROL

The definitive inventory records of most stores these days are held on a computer database, either locally or centrally, but this hasn't eliminated the paperwork, nor should it. A good stores is a very dynamic animal and a few control forms are an excellent means of recording all the facts which can then be entered into the database as and when time permits during the day. But the forms should be kept to a minimum, perhaps just one, to record any movement either in or out.

STOCK ADJUSTMENTS

A well run Stores must be one of the most dynamic areas in any company; for this reason alone control is paramount. A badly run Stores can tie up vast sums of capital and in return nullify any progress the rest of your efforts may be making towards Customer Satisfaction. For this reason some procedure has to be built into your system to remove, or drastically reduce, stock for which there is little or no demand. You need to have some process by which you are able to determine what items are clearly increasing in demand. I've seen this done in a number of ways; automatically when there is a computerised system in place, and one method which I rather liked was to let the "customer" make out a request form if they felt some new item should be added to the available inventory, or increased in the quantity currently held.

BACK-UP OF RECORDS

If you have your stock control on a computer system, remember that even the best of them do break down from time to time. You need to have some process in place to handle the possibility of:

- The data-base holding the known inventory being corrupted and in need of recovery. A daily "back-up" should be mandatory as a safeguard within the local procedures.

- There is always the possibility that for whatever reason you may from time to time lose access to the data-base. For this reason your procedures should provide for a "manual" process as an interim measure.

QUALITY RECORDS

INTRODUCTION

You should have a section in your Quality Procedures to set out clearly what are, by definition, classed as Quality Records. It should describe the retention period and how, and by whom, a record should be stored. I personally favour the idea that the Quality Manager should define which records are to be retained and as such should be sent to, and held by, the Quality Manager.

The requirement set out in the Standard is that a method must be established which will enable your company to demonstrate, with ease, that it has been satisfying its own Quality System and the conditions of BS 5750. If I were to be asked how far back such records should go, then the simple answer is 12 months, or better still, the current year plus the last full year. There is one exception to this rule of thumb, and that is records pertaining to the calibration of measuring instruments; these should be available for the previous 3 years.

You don't need to keep every related scrap of evidence; this could rapidly fill untold numbers of filing cabinets. You only need to be able to demonstrate that all elements of the Quality System were carried through to a satisfactory conclusion. Let us take, for example, a customer complaint which was successfully resolved over 12 months ago. If I were auditing this area I would not necessarily expect to find all the letters which went to and fro, or the minutes from the various meetings. I would be satisfied with a single-sheet Customer Complaint Record (like the Q1402) which gave me a potted history of the problem and notes of key events which finally produced a solution.

WHAT RECORDS TO KEEP

This really is largely up to your own judgement; with the single exception of calibration records, BS 5750 is not specific, but common sense should enable you to decide. Additionally, what records you do eventually decide to retain should be both secure and filed in such a way that they are readily retrievable. As a guide to which records I feel you should retain, I would suggest the following:

● All completed audit report forms.
● Evidence of completed Corrective Action.

- Resolved Customer Complaints.
- Product test records.
- Subcontractor performance.
- Proof of calibration (spanning 3 years).
- Proof of frequent checks on electrostatic protection facilities.
- Local Quality of Work checks.
- Stock control.
- Drawings.
- Circuit diagrams.
- Changes to documentation.
- Statistical performance.
- Back levels of software.

This list is by no means definitive, you must draw up your own, based on your own organisation's Quality System. What you have to be able to do, when asked to prove that any particular element of your Quality System is working, is produce documented evidence to demonstrate that it is.

INTERNAL QUALITY AUDITS

INTRODUCTION

Internal Auditing is the lubricant that makes the whole Quality System work. Without effective Auditing your Quality System will largely fall into disuse in next to no time. With sensibly planned Auditing the System will grow and become more and more effective.

You shouldn't rush in with some ill-throught-out scheme. It's not until you have clearly decided how your business is to operate within your Quality System, that can you really start giving some thought as to how you are going to "police" it. I use the word "police" to be deliberately provocative. But it's a good word for what is expected of you. You have hopefully installed a regime which is for both the betterment of your company and the service it provides to the customers. Additionally, and it is a big plus, if you have got it right then you can expect a smoother life for the employees and hence a happier workforce. Now all you have to do is monitor the system to make sure that people are sticking to the rules. The Standard also makes the very sensible demand on a company that the internal audits should be scheduled in relation to the importance of the activity being examined. The starting point then is to draw up a plan that will help you schedule the audits across the year and allow you to see how you are tracking against that plan. I prefer some form of matix which shows you at a glance the whole picture. A wall chart like the one below can be quite helpful in tracking the activity:

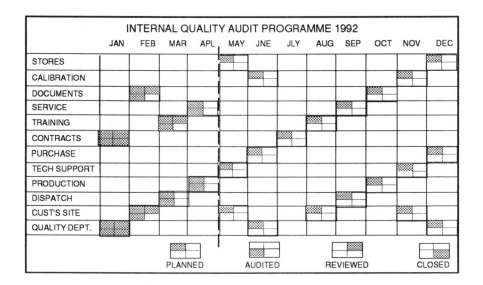

The key to a good Quality Auditing process can be summarised in a few simple points:

1.   As with any well conducted interview, the secret is *preparation*. Know who you are going to see, what their responsibilites are, and most important of all - *have a plan*.

2.   Always aim to put the auditee at ease. It can feel very intimidating, so be polite and understanding.

3.   Give the greatest auditing attention to those areas which have the greatest potential to do harm if they are allowed to go wrong.

4.   If a section of your business demonstrates its commitment to the Quality System by its evident control, then reward it by extending the period between audits.

5.   Rule 5 is the inverse of Rule 4.

6.   Focus your audits on the Quality System as installed in your company. Don't let your enthusiasm spill over into areas such as costs, morale or the state of the decorations. These may be important but the question is, are they relevant?

7.   If there is any doubt about a point then the auditee gets the benefit.

I have heard Quality described as a "moving target" and I would concede that there is a certain value in this definition. *Moving* - in that what may be acceptable Quality today may not reach the level of acceptability tomorrow. As long as one has a visible *target* its mobility is not a problem.

There are a number of methods you might choose to use when carrying out an Internal Quality Audit so let us examine them:-

FUNCTION AUDIT

This is perhaps the most common method where one department or section of a department is examined. The object of this form of audit is mainly to see how closely to the Standard and the Company procedures they operate. The advantage of this method is that generally the function being audited has well defined management boundaries and therefore there are not likely to be too many unresolved situations. By that I mean one can normally identify who "owns" a discrepancy at the time of the Audit. The disadvantage of Function Auditing is that it sees only a thin slice of The Quality System, with little attention to what happens to the product before or after the department has added its particular value to it. But don't let me fire you up with pessimism; Function Audits have their place in the Internal Auditing process. All I am saying is, don't restrict your method of monitoring the health of the system to them alone.

PROCESS AUDIT

If you feel you need to refresh your memory as to what is meant by a "Process" then return to Topic 4.9 *(p. 71)* for a quick recap. Process auditing is, I believe, the best way to get a handle on what is actually happening in a company. You will need to have a carefully drawn up plan to help keep you on track.

This method of internal quality auditing might be better understood if I were to describe a simple case. I might as the Quality Manager have a whole menu of possible processes that I can select from; here are are just a few possible examples:

- The process that gets a new part ordered, delivered and then placed into stock on the shelves of stores.

- The step-by-step process that takes place from the time a customer rings your company to report that they have a faulty item of equipment covered by a Service Contact, to the time the Service Engineer reports that he has corrected the fault.

- The process in your Training Department from the agreed requirement for a new course to teach a new product, right through to the completion of the pilot class.

We might select to carry out our Process Audit on the last example, that of the Training Department. One would need to do some preliminary background work, and a good place to start would be to see what the Training Department Procedure for developing a new training package has to say about the task. Next we will need to select a product which has completed the full cycle in recent times. Another useful part of my preparation would be to read through the records of what was found the last time this process was audited. I would be be jotting down a few questions like:

- How much notice was there prior to the first customer shipment?
- Did they get a predicted number of student places in, say, the first year?

- Was a guideline given as to the expected or acceptable length of the course?
- What guideline is there on the ratio of preparation time to course length and did it get the prescribed preparation?
- How were the instructors and course developers trained?
- Was the pilot course subjected to a detailed post-evaluation?
- Did any weaknesses get corrected?

So, armed with my prepared forms (Q1701 and Q1702 *pp. 198 and 199*), a copy of the most up-to-date version of the relevant procedure, and my check-list, I'm ready to visit the Training Department and make a start. It will put the Training Manager in a more cooperative mood if I start by describing my intention. I would tell him that I would like to follow through one "new" course from the proposal to run it, to the evaluation of the effectiveness of the pilot. The sequence of the Audit would in general follow the steps described in their own documented procedure for new course development, so I have, in this instance, a kind of road map I can follow.

It would seem to me that anything to do with a process as important as the developing and running of a new course should have been well documented and the records should be retrievable. So I'm not going to be satisfied with verbal evidence. If I can modify a famous line of Sam Goldwyn,"Verbal evidence isn't worth the paper it's written on".

I would start by taking a look at the Instructor's teaching material. I'd be looking to see what the course objectives were and how was it confirmed that the trainees achieved them - by practical tests or some sort of exam? Did the training call for practical "hands-on" sessions, and were these included? Did the students get an opportunity to evaluate the standard of material and teaching? Since this was the first course of a possible series, I would expect management to have shown interest and to have carried out some evaluation, so where is the evidence of this? There would be so much one could investigate, it would be more a case of restricting oneself rather than running out of ideas.

PATH AUDITING

In many ways Path Auditing, as I have chosen to call it, is somewhat akin to the Process Auditing I have just described, in that you don't need to restrict yourself to the boundaries of a department. But, additionally, with Path Auditing you don't even restrict your interest to a single process. Here you simply allow your curiosity to carry you down any trail that appears interesting, turning over any suspect stones in your path. The only problem with this approach is that it can be time-consuming and you can keep turning into culs-de-sac. I recall one successful Path Audit where I followed the history of a service call taken earlier in the year by a Field Service Engineer. The steps went along like this:

1.   Records showed that the engineer fixed the problem by fitting a new part.

2.   I investigated what happened to the faulty part when it was returned to the company's Stores.

3.   I next checked that the faulty item was despatched to the manufacturer for repair.

4.   A few checks demonstrated the item's eventual return back into good stock following its "repair". It was identified by serial number.

5.   As a test I had it put into a machine to see how it performed and found it immediately exhibited the identical machine malfunction the engineer had diagnosed on the original service call!

What was satisfying about this investigation was the completeness of the record keeping. Every piece of information about the service call, the movements of the part, dates, people involved, were all there or easily obtainable. It was a pity that I couldn't at the time inspect the manufacturer's testing procedures to see what their records revealed. That might have been interesting in view of the item's performance following its "repair"!

But as I stated previously, auditing in this manner can be time-consuming and also very frustrating, particularly when a path you were following comes to a dead end.

QUALITY SYSTEM REVIEWS

The Internal Quality Audit programme should form a major item in the Quality System Review. The trends in discrepancies up or down are usually good indicators of improvements (or the inverse). But it should be possible to detect, when reviewing the "big picture", those areas of the Standard which need particular attention across the company. Maybe it's Documentation, or perhaps Training; you will only be able to tell if you subject what you are finding to some Statistical analysis across a reasonable time-span.

LOCUM AUDITORS

I know of very few companies with enough full-time staff in the Quality Department to run an effective, comprehensive, Internal Auditing programme within their own resources. But this is no impediment to success and can turn out to be a strength. What is required is a pool of designated managers across the various departments who can be called upon to carry out audits. The Quality Manager will need to be certain of this resource and I would recommend that each of these managers should assign certain days across the year which the Quality Manager can build into his schedule. The training of these "helpers" needs to be considered.

Using the line management to carry out Internal Audits has many advantages. They develop a better understanding of the requirements of the Standard, and see new ways of applying it. They get to know how other units of the company work and they pick up good ideas which they can take back and incorporate into their own operation. It also improves general communications across the company. You will, however, need to provide training for auditors, both the full-time people and any "locums" you enlist. So let us examine this matter of training your internal auditors.

AUDITOR TRAINING

The Standard requires that everyone should have undergone training to enable them to carry out the duties they are called upon to perform. This must be particularly true in the case of those people who are called upon to monitor the health of your Quality System. There are a number of options available to you and what is best for your company is, of course, for you to decide. An outside training organisation is one possibility, but these courses are not inexpensive and are sometimes designed around the more specialised role of "assessment"; assessment being to examine the total working of a company to see that it meets the requirements laid down in the Standard. The Quality Manager should certainly have attended such an "external" course, as should anyone else on your staff who has a predominant role in preparing the company for its formal assessment. I would also suggest that any full-time auditors assigned to the Quality Department following your accreditation should likewise be given the benefit of formal training.

You will find, at the end of this topic, a list of training organisations who specialise in Quality-related training. Many of these organisations provide a specific "industry" focus to their teaching, since they have the specialisation background to enable them to tailor their courses and so match the requirements of BS 5750 to a client's commercial sector interests. Once you have this core of formally trained people, one of their objectives should be to provide training to others on your staff who are called upon from time to time to carry out audits on behalf of the Quality Department. As I pointed out earlier, what might be required is a selection of "locum" line managers who, with suitable training, could confirm by surveillance inspections that the various functions around the company are complying with the Quality System. Local training, prepared and given by your own Quality Department, would not only seem quite acceptable but even desirable, since they know the various departments within your company and they know the Quality System your Company has put in place. A final point regarding the training of these "helper" auditors - do make sure that not only have they been appropriately trained but there is a record of their training on file; you are sure to be asked for it one day.

CHECK-LISTS

The secret of a successful interview of any sort is *preparation* and to that end I am a great believer in the assistance of check-lists when carrying out audits. Clearly the check-list has to be prepared to match the area of responsibility one is about to visit; have a look at the sample Work Instruction - Quality Audit Checklist for a Field Engineer I have included in Part 3 *(p. 205)*. This would be just one of many Work Instruction sheets and I would expect the Quality Department to have prepared one for each function likely to be inspected.

Such lists aren't intended to be totally comprehensive, but rather point the auditor at one or two key areas they really should inspect on every visit, while listing other options they could select from. I still sometimes find myself, despite having carried out many hundreds of audits, having a mental block in the middle of an interview and that's when I am thankful that I have a check-list I can fall back on.

CONCLUSION OF AN AUDIT

No matter how long the audit takes, you will need to allocate some time at the end to make some summary notes and to get a signed agreement to any discrepancies you have uncovered. Take a look at the Q1701 and Q1702 forms that I have provided *(pp. 198 and 199);* you will notice that they both call for the signed agreement of both the auditor and auditee. Experience has taught me that when you leave the auditee's office you should have reached total agreement regarding the discrepancies (if there were any) and all the paperwork should have been completed. I like to leave the auditee a copy of the total report.

A point regarding the presentation of any discrepancies you leave with the auditee; try in your write-up to leave them with a factual description of exactly what was observed - where, what, who, etc. Also, stick to local terminology. Finally, try to be helpful, but you would be wise not to offer solutions; the problem is *theirs* and you should let them decide how they intend fixing it.

FOLLOW-UP ACTIVITY

There is still some closing business to complete by the Quality Department. Firstly, they need to have some form of day-file or wall chart which will give them notice of any agreed target dates for the clearing of discrepancies. They also need to give some thought as to when the next audit of that particular section will take place. Maybe the intervals between audits can be extended if things looked good, or perhaps the inverse is more apt. It is also possible that the audit just completed has revealed a weakness in some other department in which case a Corrective Action needs to be raised. The only guidance I can give you is to complete this final administration quickly before memories fade, say within 48 hours.

AUDITOR TRAINING

The following UK organisations run training courses on Quality Assurance and BS 5750:

GEC Management College
Dunchurch, Rugby, Warwickshire.
Tele: 0788-814198
Fax: 0788-814451

BSI Quality Assurance
Training Service,
BSI Quality Assurance, PO Box 375,
Milton Keynes MK14 6LL.
Tel: 0908-220908
Fax: 0908-220671

Gilbert Associates (Europe) Ltd
Fraser House, 15 London Road,
Twickenham,
Middlesex TW1 3ST.
Tele: 081-891-4383
Fax: 081-891-5885

AMTAC Laboratories Ltd
Norman Road, Broadheath,
Altrincham,
Cheshire WA14 4EP.
Tel: 061-928-8924
Fax: 061-927-7359

Stebbing and Partners
1 Coppice Wood, West Ashton Road,
Trowbridge Wiltshire BA14 6DW.
Tel/Fac: 0225-754946

Quality Consultant Services Ltd
Suite 702, Fleming House, 2 Tryst Road,
Cumbernauld, Glasgow G69 1JW.
Tel: 0236-73447
Fax: 0236-725070

The Institute of Quality Assurance
10 Grosvenor Gardens,
London SW1W 0DQ.
Tel: 071-730-7154

David Hutchins Associates Ltd
13/14 Hermitage Parade,
High Street, Ascot,
Berkshire SL5 7HE.
Tel: 0344-28712
Fax: 0344-25968

Bywater
119 Guildford Street, Chertsey,
Surrey KT16 9AL.
Tel: 0932-567866
Fax: 0932- 568157

Campden
(Food & Drink Research
Association)
Chipping Campden, Gloucestershire
GL55 6LD.
Tel: 0386-840319
Fax: 0386-841360

Yarsley Quality Assured Firms Ltd
Trowers Way, Redhill,
Surrey RH1 2JN.
Tel: 0737-768445
Fax: 0737-761229

Irish Quality Association
Merrion Hall, Strand Road,
Sandymount, Dublin 4.
Tel: (010-353) 1-2695255
Fax: (010-353) 1-2695820

TRAINING

There are quite a number of different levels of training which would satisfy the Standard; it certainly doesn't all have to be formal "classroom" style. The weakness one usually finds when examining training within a company is not that people are performing tasks for which they have not been trained, but that there is no record anywhere to illustrate what instruction they have had. There is seldom any difficulty if their training was through attending a formal course; one can usually find evidence of this, sometimes with some form of certificate issued by the training organisation. More frequently, however, the training given to staff tends to be informal and in the nature of supervised "on the job" experience. There is absolutely nothing wrong with this; it can be the most effective way to teach some skills. But all too often one finds that it was unstructured, and there is no record to demonstrate that it was ever completed.

The initial introductory training which new employees take during the first few weeks on joining your company is crucial. There needs to be a definitive list of all those elements they need to know to operate efficiently in the company. The listing of what needs to be covered could be expanded to serve as both a schedule and a record, along the lines of a Control Sheet, as shown below.

Employee's Name		Manager's Name	
Topic	Date	Given by	Employee's signature
Company intro			
Company ethics			
Health & Safety			
BUPA			
Data protection			
Electrostatic			
Products			
Quality System			
Customer contact			
On-line mail			
All elements satisfactorily completed			
Employee .... Manager...................... Date......................			

Sample Training Control Sheet

If I was auditing a department and looking into the training given to staff, let me list the route I would take, since this should direct your thinking into the comprehensiveness of your training programme. I would be asking the questions:-

- Is there a company Procedure to guide management on the topic of Training and is this department following it?

- Have they a basic minimum set of modules which everyone must complete, including such elements as Safety at Work, Departmental Organisation, Protection of Data, etc?

- Have the various special training requirements for the different jobs within the department been defined?

- Are there people in the department assigned to carry out local training, and have they had proven training in teaching such skills?

- If there are prerequisites to certain courses, how does one find out what they are?

- Is there a proper guide of what should be taught? In other words, is there a detailed syllabus for each module?

- Is there an overall Training Plan available for each member of the department and is there evidence of it being observed?

- Is there an up-to-date record of where each member of the staff is currently placed in the programme of training mapped out for them?

- Has it been defined who is designated to ensure staff are trained, allocate course places and maintain records?

- Does any evaluation of the effectiveness of the training take place?

- Is the student's performance evaluated in any way, say by examination or practical tests on completion of the course?

SERVICING

INTRODUCTION

Servicing is one of the shortest clauses in the Standard, in fact a solitary 24 word sentence, but its implications for some companies is quite considerable. Many manufacturing companies run their own Customer Service and Repair organisations, while there are many examples of companies these days who provide maintenance service for other manufacturer's products. A careful consideration, then, of Servicing is essential because it is a vast and complicated matter whose mismanagement can wreck your Quality System before it gets off the ground.

Let's develop a Service Department and step by step see what it needs to function efficiently while at the same time meeting the requirements of the Standard.

INCOMING REQUESTS FOR SERVICE (CALL RECEIPT)

Ideally, this needs to be a dedicated function. However, in a small company with only a handful of calls a day, it might have to be invested in the telephone switchboard operator or the front office receptionist. But in our sample company we could have hundreds of calls coming in each day and we will need a staff of, let us say five people to receive these calls. Now let us consider what we need to provide these people with:

- A current list of customers, which should indicate both the equipment the customer has installed and some way that the taker of the service request can know what contractual agreement, if any, there is with our company.
- A means of recording the details of the request, tracking its progress and recording information about the final resolution. If you are to handle hundreds of calls you will rapidly fill shelves with paper and you will find even a simple database programme running on a PC may be the better option. This would simplify the analysis of your performance, which is a requirement of the Standard anyway. As guidance I have provided a form which you might choose to modify for this purpose (See Form E1901, *p. 189*).
- You might consider providing the staff with some simple aide memoire to deal with the call so as to ensure it was handled courteously while still getting all the relevant information quickly and efficiently.

125

Once the details of the requirement have been taken, you are faced with a number of options. How are you to handle the despatching of the engineer? One way, providing they have the skills, is to let the people who accepted the call also despatch it. This might be efficient if they have the technical knowledge to understand fully the nature of the customer's problem. It is my experience that a better solution is to keep receipt and despatch separated. Then you can optimise the use of the technically skilled people to both diagnose the problem and, as is frequently the case, fix the problem there and then over the phone. Customers, contrary to popular belief, have been known to be wrong in that they were using the equipment incorrectly. Moreover, this level of communication has the advantage that the customer is generally impressed when talking to someone who clearly understands the equipment and its applications.

CALL DESPATCH

So, in our model company we have decided to keep receipt and despatch separate, and the incoming request, once it has been registered, needs to be passed on to a dedicated, preferably technical, person to analyse. They should have enough knowledge to establish if this is a *real* malfunction of the equipment or simply misuse. They may be able to offer the customer a temporary solution over the telephone, and so take the urgency out of the situation. My preference would be to instigate a roster, so that each of the actual customer site attending engineers gets some exposure to this remote form of service activity. You would probably have to assign one full-time, dedicated person to Call Despatch so that the facilities are properly maintained and enhanced.

The Call Despatcher needs always to question whether it is a "real fault" or simply incorrect use. Can it be fixed by the customer with a little guidance? Can the customer carry out any tests or run some diagnostics to give a clearer definition of the problem? Will the engineer need to take items to site, like special tools or parts? What is the severity of the problem from the customer's point of view?

Very often an early dialogue with the user will resolve the problem there and then. This would be both to the satisfaction of the customer and cost saving to your company. If it can be resolved over the telephone this will also help your measured performance in statistical terms.

Technology employed in many large pieces of customer equipment, such as computer mainframes, incorporate remote diagnostic support. This enables the Service Despatch engineer to run sophisticated tests over a telephone line with little or no intervention by anyone at the customer location. So here is yet another reason for having technical people available in the "customer support" function.

SUPPORTING THE ENGINEER

This is a major part of the Service Receipt and Despatch facility and again, if run well is not only a major element in customer satisfaction but can reduce the "on-site" time of the engineer. The technician who analyses the nature of the problem is in a good position to estimate what the engineer visiting the customer may additionally need. Some companies find it cost-efficient, for example, for the engineer to have available a "kit" with all the major or most frequently failing items. It may be possible to intelligently deduce the exact component needed. In all these situations it would seem good practice to either make sure the engineer takes the parts with him or to send the spares on to the the customer's site ahead of the engineer. The practice of sending certain spares on ahead of the engineer impresses the customer enormously.

Another advantage in operating a technically knowledgeable Service Despatch is the assistance over the telephone that can be given to the engineer while he is "on site" investigating the problem. The technician back at base can have more technical documentation available to him and maybe a file of "known fault" information, with the ability to search on the parameter of symptoms. All this material might be too bulky, too confidential or simply impractical to hold at each site.

Special tools, test sets, oscilloscopes and so on can also be more sensibly managed by the Service Despatch. This way you simply need to despatch out to the engineer the equipment he might require as and when its need becomes apparent from the nature of the fault. As I posed elsewhere in this book, why have every engineer carry an expensive and annually calibrated meter around just so that once or twice a year he has it available to set up a voltage? I would always examine the feasibility of giving people the minimum they need in order to carry out their duties, but provide a reliable service which can deliver to them on site anything they might deem necessary, task by task.

RESPONSE AND CLEAR TIME

This will depend to a large extent on what your contractual obligations are to your customers. But let me first define a few terms since there is, I find, frequently some confusion in meaning.

Response time is the lapsed time between the customers placing their problem with your staff and a trained engineer arriving on site and starting work on the fault. Customers frequently make the mistake of being impressed by a quick response time to a call. It may be a comfort having a Service Engineer on the premises, but I would have thought it would be more comforting having the equipment repaired and back in use. A service organisation can improve the "response time" simply by sending any engineer who happens to be free at the time rather than waiting until the most skilled man is available.

Fix time is the length of time it takes the engineer to rectify the fault. This generally indicates either the skill of the engineer or the availability of spare parts.

Clear time (or Down time) is the total time which the equipment was unavailable to the user. This is what really matters. After all, your customer's purpose in having the equipment installed at his premises is so that it is available to help serve his business needs, so the shorter the Clear Time the better.

Temporary clear time is the time taken to get the equipment back into a usable state although not yet fully repaired (e.g. awaiting a new part).

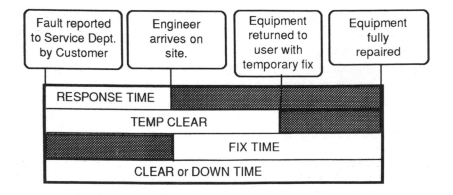

The diagram above shows graphically the various distinctions

PER-CALL SERVICE

It also logically follows that the people handling the customer service requests on the telephone in the Service Dept do actually *know*, by whatever means, what your company's contractual obligations are for each call made on your engineering Service. They should also have clear instructions as regards requests for Service from owners of equipment who don't have any formal contract, but would like your company to come out and repair their faulty equipment on a "time and materials" basis. Some Service organisations refer to this as a "Per-Call Service".

TRAINED ENGINEERS

The Standard seeks to ensure that you only deploy trained personnel on the servicing of equipment or software (see Part 1 Topic 4.18). It is not simply enough to have engineers trained; you have to be able to demonstrate that the people responding to the customers' requests on the telephone in the Service Dept are aware of who has been trained on which products. Something along the lines of a "training matrix" is an acceptable way of satisfying this need, but do ensure that it is kept up to date.

SYSTEM BACK-UP

Most companies these days use a PC or some form of "on-line" database system to hold the information needed by Service Requests and the Service Despatch of requests. Make sure that your procedures clearly show operators both:

1. How they should handle the requests and the despatch of engineers in the event of the system being unavailable (loss of power or fault on the equipment).
2. That the data held in such a system is "backed up" at frequent intervals.

SERVICE REQUEST RECORDS

You will find two forms (E1901 and E1902 *pp. 189 and 190*) in Part 3 of this book which, if not directly appropriate to your company's needs, could be simply adapted. E1901 is for the people in the office receiving the request from the customers to note down all the particulars as they are given over the telephone. Even if there is an electronic data-gathering system for the reception of customer requests it is frequently helpful to be able to jot down some of the information by hand - we are not all "touch" typists you know! You will notice that I have provided a box at the foot of E1901 so that you can denote once the information has been fully entered into whatever electronic database you are using.

A form such as E1901 is going to be essential anyway if only as a "back-up" in the event of your electronic system being out of service for whatever reason.

The next point to consider is what record are you going to generate from the user end of the Service Request. Have a look at the form E1902. It is intended that the visiting service engineer will raise this form at the completion of his visit to site, and its purpose is fourfold:

1.   It provides a fairly comprehensive "hard-copy" record of what exactly happened on site - dates, times, parts, people involved, etc.

2.   It is signed by the customer to indicate that he agrees the problem has been fully resolved and he confirms the time and date the equipment was returned to him.

3.   It declares whether the activity is going to be invoiced since it indicates if there is or isn't a Service Contract to cover the work.

4.   The lower section of the form invites the customer to give, by means of a few ticks, his impression of the service he has received. I realise that this section will not always be practical, for example, if the customer has a large base of equipment under contract and your engineers are on site almost daily.

The link between this form (E1902) and the Service Request Record (E 1901) is the Job Number. This is a sequential number issued by by the Call Receipt people when the problem was initially reported. I would expect eventually to find the E1901 and E1902 for each service call to be brought together and stored for a precribed period. The "Customer Impression" information gathered from the E1902 can be collated to provide, say, a monthly representative snap-shot of the general level of satisfaction with the Service you are providing.

STATISTICAL TECHNIQUES

GOOD AND BAD STATISTICS

They say there are lies, damned lies and statistics. Whatever your own personal attitude may be towards statistics the Standard does require that your company makes, where appropriate, some intelligent use of statistical techniques to evaluate the effectiveness (or otherwise) of your product or service. Don't fall into the all-too-often observed practice of producing pretty charts that say virtually nothing and mistakenly claim them to be elegant statistics. I have found many companies who use statistics like a drunk uses a lamp-post, more for support than illumination, let me lay down a few ground rules which you might be wise to keep in mind.

Keep them simple and don't fall into the habit of tracking parameters simply because the numbers are easy to obtain. I am also of the opinion that there are only three sample sizes in statistical analysis, too small, too large and just right. I see too many charts which only serve to confuse and blur the truth, rather than reveal it. Go for quality, precision and relevance, rather than quantity and questionable parameters. Avoid the all-too-common practice of masking the true trends by modifying the parameters. If the answers being provided by your statistics are unpalatable, don't fall into the trap of changing the questions.

Look for continuing trends, not momentary blips. There is a whole science to statistical analysis and one of its key purposes is to discover if a process is under control. Over-reacting to a momentary blip can do more harm than good. The question should be *"is it under control?"* If the answer is "Yes", then leave it for the moment, but continue to monitor. Having said that, one should not lose sight of the fact that statistical measurement and analysis in themselves will not fix anything. It is the intelligent use of the results in terms of action that brings about improvement. Finally, in the business world there is generally not a lot of profit in measuring and charting effects which you can't influence.

The only true purpose of a good statistical chart is either to reveal that some desirable characteristic is remaining stable or getting better, or alternatively, that some undesirable characteristic is in need of positive intervention. Gathering good unpolluted data can be both time-consuming and expensive. For these reasons alone you should ensure that you are gathering the right information and, moreover, making the optimum use of it. Let me give you an example which may help illustrate my point.

A Salutary tale

One very large company was concerned about the number of complaints being made by their customers regarding the difficulty they were having when attempting to telephone the Service Department about equipment requiring an engineer's attention. The Service organisation quite rightly realised that the speed at which they answered the telephone when a customer rang with a request for service was a major factor in the customer's perception of the Quality of the service.

Their internal telephone exchange was modern, and so able to measure and provide reports showing the delay between an incoming caller being able to hear a ringing tone and the telephone being answered by one of their staff. They set themselves what they thought was a reasonable target. This aimed for 85% of all calls to be answered within 25 seconds. The next step was to measure what the delay was "today". They used a representative data sample by logging every incoming call during two busy time slots each day.

Within a couple of weeks they had enough data to demonstrate that the target of 85% was not being achieved and employed an additional "temp" to improve the answering time. They went on to measure for a further 2 weeks to confirm the effectiveness of their solution and the figures levelled out within a point or so of the desired 85%. And that, they thought, had fixed the problem. The truth was that, contrary to their belief, they hadn't begun to understand the problem, let alone solve it.

For a start, many of the disgruntled incoming callers were simply putting the telephone down, rather than wait for 25 seconds, and because of the way the telephone exchange worked, these calls never got into the statistics. And what about 25 seconds, is that a reasonable target time? I wondered if they had even sampled for themselves how it feels to wait on the end of an unanswered telephone for nearly half a minute. Furthermore, if I have waited all that time to get the phone answered, then I'd want to talk to someone who could deal with my problem there and then, not just hear somebody ask me to "hold" until someone else becomes free to talk to me. The way they were handling these incoming callers meant it was the poor customers who were not only being made to waste their time, but also having to pay for the privilege of the silent "holding on". At least before the *"improvements"* the customers got to listen to "ringing tone" for free! But statistically the Service organisation could prove they had fixed the problem!

Getting back to the general topic of statistics, I believe you should be able to demonstrate that you are providing what you are selling. If your contract with the customer specifies a response time to his request for an engineer "on-site" in 4 hours, then you had better find some way of reliably measuring it. Likewise total "down time" should be carefully monitored and tracked statistically.

IS IT UNDER CONTROL?

The true purpose of statistics is to determine whether a process is under control. Resist the temptation to tamper with contributary factors unless you have indisputable evidence that to do so will effect a permanent and worthwhile improvment. Or, as the Americans so precisely put it -"If it ain't broke, don't fix it".

There is a management tool called "Statistical Quality Control", beyond the scope of this book, which I would recommend you investigate. It provides, amongst other techniques, a means of plotting performance against acceptable limits of variation. One chart which you can produce allows you to observe some variable parameter against acceptable upper and lower limits. If the chart goes outside the lower limit in three consecutive samples or just once outside the upper limit - then and only then do you investigate and take some corrective action.

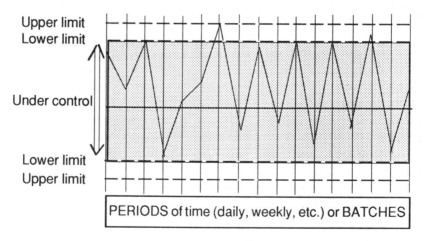

A Statistical Quality Control chart

Part 2

New Era plc

Sample Quality Manual

Copy Number	

New Era plc - QUALITY MANUAL

This Sample Quality Manual could be used as the foundation of such an item of documentation by any Manufacturing and/or Service company. You need to keep in mind that the Quality Manual is not a book of instruction, it is an overall statement of policy. It needs to say *what* is to happen within your Quality System, not *how*.

In practice, only a limited number of Quality Manuals are provided across a company, and these are usually found to be held by the senior managers of the major departments. It is only necessary for the staff to know where a copy can be found should they need it for reference at any time.

In essence, the purpose of the Quality Manual is to describe, in broad terms, how the clauses of BS 5750 are to be interpreted by your company. If a clause of the Standard doesn't apply to your company then simply exclude it; there is no point in trying to incorporate clauses which don't enter into your company's business. You may, for example, never have the purchasers of *your* product supply *you* with materials towards the manufacturing process, or perhaps your company is a manufacturing organisation and doesn't provide a "Maintenance Service" on your products. In such situations, then just omit those particular clauses.

I have kept the overall design of the manual as uncluttered as I can, and I would advise that you do the same. The page "banner" is simple and uniform, yet it supplies you with all the information you need. The method used for page numbering is by placing a plus behind the number if there is another page to follow; and a minus on the last page of the set. The section numbering of the manual has been arranged so that it directly cross-relates to the applicable clause of the Standard, and with the text of Part 1.

The page "banners" in this Quality Manual also contain an Issue Number which enables the reader to check to see if they are reading the most up-to-date version. The Issue Numbers on each page should match with the current Issue Control Matrix information *(p. 141)*.

Just one final point with regard to changes or additions you'll need to make from time to time to your documentation. I like to see such alterations brought to the reader's attention in some way; the "bar" to the left of a paragraph is one way of indicating an alteration from the previous issue of the page. *(see p. 168)*.

From: The office of the Chairman and Managing Director of New Era plc.

To: All employees.

Wednesday 6th May 1992.

Ladies and Gentlemen,

In accordance with the wishes of the Management Board of New Era plc, the company has undertaken to seek registration with the British Standards Institution to BS 5750 - Part 1. In making this decision New Era plc propose to implement and maintain a Quality System throughout all areas of its business activities.

Business and industries throughout the world will reward the Quality of New Era plc by continuing to place orders for our products and services. It is, however, essential that we all are aware that the responsibility for the Quality image of New Era plc rests with each and every member of the company. It is only by our joint effort and total continuing commitment to Quality in everything we do that we will achieve the high standard we are seeking.

Quality is not only the destination but the route. We must be constantly seeking ways to improve each and every process within our company; only in this way will we continue to enhance our products and the service we provide to our customers. Every member of the company will shortly attend a training session to have explained to them the "New Era Quality System". Similarly, all new employees on joining the company will be trained in this way before they are assigned any formal duties.

The "Ownership" of the New Era Quality System resides with myself as your Managing Director. I have appointed to the Management Board a Quality Manager who will report directly to me and will have total responsibility to manage and direct all matters relating to Quality in our Company. His position within the Management Board should serve to indicate the high priority this venture has been given.

I am confident I have the support of you all.

Yours sincerely

John P. Aldridge
Chairman & Managing Director of New Era plc

A copy of this letter should be placed at the beginning of the Quality Manual

Copy No [   ]   e = empty from here   ◯ = changed this issue

Sec	Page	1	2	3	4	5	6	7
0	Issue control matrix	(4)	4	e				
1	Management	1	e					
2	Quality system	1	e					
3	Contract review	1	2	e				
4	Design control	2	e					
5	Document control	1	1	e				
6	Purchasing	3	2	e				
7	Purchaser supplied	3	e					
8	Product identification	1	e					
9	Process control	1	e					
10	Inspection and testing	2	e					
11	Measure & test equipment	1	e					
12	Inspection & test status	2	e					
13	Nonconforming product	2	(3)	e				
14	Corrective action	3	e					
15	Handling, packing, etc.	2	2	e				
16	Quality records	1	e					
17	Internal quality audits	1	e					
18	Training	1	e					
19	Servicing	1	e					
20	Statistics	1	e					

Copies of this manual have been issued to the following people:

Copy No	Holder	Position
1	J P Aldridge	Managing Director
2 (Master)	G Anderson	Quality Manager
3	P D Wellmaker	Head of Marketing
4	J Smith	Head of Production
5	A W Brewer	Head of Engineering
6	S Faraday	Head of Development and Design
7	V Thomas	Head of Logistics

UPDATES

Updated pages for this Quality Manual will always include a revised copy of this section. Upon receipt please *insert the new pages,* including the new Section 4.0 (Issue control matrix) into your copy of the Quality Manual.

Complete the form below and *return this actual page* to the Quality Manager as confirmation that your copy of the Quality Manual has been brought up to the latest issue.

Please destroy the old pages that you removed.

Thank you.

_____

I confirm that the most recent updates to the Quality Manual have been inserted into my copy:

Name .... Signature ....

Internally mail this whole original page to:

Quality Manager, Room 23, Blockwell House.

OVERVIEW

The aim of New Era plc is to provide high quality products and service to its customers whilst maintaining efficiency and profitability. It is management responsibility at all levels within the company to ensure that Quality is not knowingly compromised and that every effort is made to continually improve both our products and the service.

THE ROLE OF MANAGEMENT

It is the responsibility of every manager to ensure that the company commitment to BS 5750 is upheld and that all departments adhere to the New Era plc documented Quality System. A comprehensive continual auditing process will be conducted by the Quality Department to monitor and enhance the Quality System.

Management are required to ensure that all company activity is in full compliance with relevant statutory and safety requirements.

All new employees will undergo Quality System training prior to being assigned any role within the company. It is the responsibility of the Training Manager to ensure that such training courses are available within two weeks of any new employee joining the company.

REVIEWS

Quality reviews are to be conducted regularly by all management on the functions within their range of responsibility. The frequency and format of these reviews are fully described in Quality Procedures.

Quality System Reviews by senior management will be held twice a year. These reviews take the form of a meeting to be chaired by the General Manager and the heads of all departments will attend. The agenda and format of these Quality System Reviews can be seen in Quality Procedures.

OVERVIEW

The New Era Quality System is the sum of all the processes and procedures described in this manual. The system is owned by the Managing Director who has appointed a Quality Manager to document, implement, monitor and continually improve the process.

SCOPE OF THE QUALITY SYSTEM

It is the responsibility of the Quality Manager to produce, maintain and monitor a documented Quality System on behalf of New Era plc. The Quality System includes..

- This Quality Manual.
- Quality Procedures.
- Departmental Procedures.
- Registered Local Procedures.
- Internal Quality Auditing Scheme.
- Corrective Action process. ←
- Concessions.
- Audits carried out by BSI.
- Quality System Training of all employees.
- *"Quality Briefing"* - a 3-monthly newsletter to all employees.
- Quality Awards.
- Work Instructions.
- Job Descriptions. *- Personnel*
- Standards of workmanship. *Specifications Control.*

Enquiries
Complaints resolved
Document Control
Root fault finding
staff Training

The Quality Manager will report directly to the Managing Director on all matters pertaining to the Quality System and the company's Registration to BS 5750 - Part 1.

The company Quality System will be formally reviewed twice a year by the company Quality Council chaired by the Managing Director.The Quality Council will be appointed by the MD and will include a senior manager from each division or department affected . This twice-a-year meeting will be known as the Quality System Review.

GENERAL

Service Contracts are the responsibility of the Engineering Director. Please refer to Quality Procedures for detailed instruction related to Service Contract Reviews.

The terms and conditions of all the standard Service Contract offerings available to our customers will be reviewed once a year for their relevance to customer requirements, the industry norm and profitability.

EXISTING SERVICE CONTRACTS

All existing Service Contracts will be reviewed annually. The review will consider the customer's current inventory and any changes to the terms and conditions which might enhance the quality and suitability of the service being provided. The Pricing Department have the responsibility to adjust the monthly invoicing in alignment with the current price list. The customer will be made aware of the conclusions of this review.

Quality Procedures will be followed in the execution of all reviews of Service Contracts.

NEW OFFERINGS

The Engineering Department are responsible for the creation of any New Offerings intended to be made generally available to our customers. Any proposed new offerings will be subjected to careful market research and detailed investigation into the company's ability to resource and profitably sustain the proposed offering. A new offering will not be made generally available until two trial contracts have been run for a minimum of 3-months and have satisfactorily passed their post-trial review.

SPECIAL SERVICE CONTRACT OFFERINGS

Special offerings are defined as those which exhibit significant variations to any of the company's current range of Standard Service Offerings.

The customer's requirements will have been fully documented by the customer and/or Marketing Department. The Pricing Department will consider a Special Service Contract if either the customer requests it or if this company considers it to be an acceptable and suitable sales incentive. Any such Special Offering must undergo a detailed review by Engineering, Marketing and Sales and, wherever possible, the customer. The customer will not be offered a Special Service or provided with a final price until all four departments have concurred.

The "3-month trial status" process required in the case of a new standard offering is not relevant in the case of a Special Offering; however, a formal review must take place within 6 months of the contract commencement date so that adjustments can be made at the time of the annual renewal date.

TASK CONTRACTS

Task contracts are defined as those where there is a single process to be performed on behalf of one specific customer. A detailed specification must be compiled by the Engineering Department from customer-supplied input. If the task is considered an acceptable, attainable requirement for which resource can be made available, then a quotation for such work is to be drafted and agreed by Engineering and Pricing Departments for presentation to the customer.

The customer may be provided with a "provisional budgetary estimate" of the probable cost. However, only the Pricing Department is permitted to issue such an estimate.

CUSTOMER NOTIFICATION

Customers must be formally notified by the Engineering Department with 1 month's notice of any changes to the terms, conditions or pricing of any Service Contract Agreements. This notification will include a new "schedule" section of the contract showing precisely the new terms and/or price. The customer will be invited to sign and return it to indicate his approval of the new schedule.

INTRODUCTION

The responsibility for the design of New Era hardware and software products is invested in the Design and Development Department. The Engineering Department is responsible for any Service Offerings made generally available to our customers.

HARDWARE AND SOFTWARE PRODUCTS

Any product added to the company portfolio must be able to match the following criteria:

1.   Present an improvement in performance and/or price to any current New Era plc offering.
2.   Be superior to any competitive equipment of similar specification currently available.
3.   Be fully supportable at the time of first customer shipment by both Field Engineering and Logistics.

SERVICE OFFERINGS

The development of New Service Offerings generally emerges from the release of new products into the marketplace and for that reason New Service Offerings are to be developed by the Engineering Department alongside the development of the product. Variations in terms and conditions to the portfolio of current Service Offerings is also the responsibility of the Engineering Department.

The Engineering Department may wish to make other non-product-related Service Offerings available, either because of a specific marketplace opportunity or as a result of some special requirement by our customers. The design of any such Special Service Contract must conform to the requirements of the appropriate Engineering Procedure and must also have the approval of the Management Board before being offered to any customer.

Prior to any formal announcement by New Era plc to add a New Product or Service Offering to the company portfolio, a design verification/evaluation trial has to have been undertaken at a limited number of agreed sites.

CONTROL

The Quality System documentation for New Era plc will be registered, produced, controlled and distributed by the Quality Department. The range of controlled documents fall into two distinct groups and are as follows:

1.   ***Company-wide***   Quality Manual
                              Quality Procedures

2.   ***Departmental***

Each department of the company is required to produce and maintain its own Departmental Operational Procedures. These Procedures must conform with the company standard format for Quality Documentation and will be both monitored and issued by the Quality Department.

Departments may produce additional Quality System documents of special value to their particular section of the company. Documents such as forms, drawings, Work Instructions, Testing Procedures and Local Procedures would fall into this category. These special departmental documents must be registered and approved by the Quality Department so as to ensure they conform to the company format. Once registered they must be maintained so as to remain current and under strict local issue control and distribution.

OWNERSHIP OF DOCUMENTS

All Quality documentation will have an assigned owner. The Quality Department will maintain a register of document owners. It is the responsibility of the owner to ensure that documents assigned to them are reviewed at sensible intervals and maintained such as to reflect the required working practice at the time of issue.

DISTRIBUTION AND AMENDMENTS

All documentation supporting the New Era plc Quality System must be registered with the Quality Department. With the exception of registered Local documentation, all amendments, additions and issuing of Quality documentation will be carried out exclusively by the Quality Department.

The process by which any changes can be initiated or new material added to the company documentation is fully described in Quality Procedures.

MASTER LIBRARY

A full set of all company Quality documentation will be held as a master library set in the Quality Department.

HISTORY

Each department, including the Quality Department, is required to retain a copy of the previous issue of any new Procedure for reference purposes.

REVIEW

The company Quality documentation will be subjected to review within the half-yearly Quality System Review.

CONTROL OF PURCHASING

Centralised purchasing enables New Era plc to obtain advantageous trading terms and delivery and the ability to control the quality of materials and services obtained from our suppliers. For these sound business reasons the responsibility for the purchasing of all goods and services is assigned to the Purchasing Department and will follow the Purchase Order Request (POR) described in Purchasing Procedures. The only permitted relaxation to this control is where the Purchasing Department has specified certain financial thresholds below which management may make local purchases. Financial Procedures describe the current Sterling levels of these thresholds.

The total annual value of purchases made from any single supplier must never exceed 10% of the supplier's sales. This regulation within New Era plc purchasing policy is to protect our suppliers in the event of us wishing to withdraw our custom from them for any reason.

PORs fall into the following categories and the POR number will always start with the *class* of the POR as follows:

Class

A	Standard order placed with a preferred supplier (PS)
B	Replenishing, repeat order with a PS
C	Established contract services
D	Trial purchase with new supplier (materials or service)
E	Any other

All Purchase Order Requests (POR) are to be formally submitted to Purchasing Department. Departments may express preferred suppliers from the current Preferred Supplier List (PSL) and this will be given consideration by the Purchasing Department. The buying department may submit a POR for specific orders to be placed with suppliers not on the PSL; in such cases the supplier may be subject, depending on the purchase value of the order, to an inspection by New Era plc to confirm their ability to supply to specification.

At the discretion of the Purchasing Department such new suppliers may be added to the PSL.

Variations to the PSL will be effected by the Purchasing Department. Twice a year a total review will take place of the PSL and a new listing issued.

Requests for the purchasing of services are to be subjected to tender against clear, precise contractual specifications. The requesting department is required to submit a detailed specification of its needs along with a POR, just as it would if ordering materials.

The management level of authorisation sign-off for POR is to be found in Financial Procedures (please refer).

SEGREGATION

Customer-supplied materials will be segregated from company-owned materials until such time as they are to be incorporated into the customer-ordered equipment.

CARE OF MATERIAL

All such items are to be stored and handled in accordance with the owner's specifications, standard safety practices and good housekeeping.

A register will be maintained in the warehouse allowing the identification, location, and in/out movements of all such material. Checks arc to be made periodically to confirm the accuracy of the register.

To whatever extent it is practically possible, all customer-owned items are to carry precise identification, as described in Quality Procedures.

LOSS OR DAMAGE

Any failure, loss or damage of such parts must be reported to the customer as soon as possible.

It has to be possible through whatever form of identification is practical, for the constituent components, parts, assemblies and sub-assemblies of all New Era plc products to be traced to their origin.

Each phase of the assembly, construction wiring and testing is fully described in the Work Instructions pertaining to the product.

There has to be a traceable record to identify the New Era plc employee responsible for each phase of the manufacture.

Records should show:

- Source of all purchased assemblies and other major items, along with proof of their suitability by evidence of prescribed testing.

- Evidence of correct construction practices being observed in New Era plc Manufacturing by both test results, where applicable, and signed off Work Instruction.

- Evidence that all prescribed final Product Function Tests and Quality Inspections have been carried out and fully meet with specification.

- All records pertaining to the manufacture, testing and inspection of New Era plc products must be retained for a period of not less than 1 year following despatch to the customer.

PROCESS OWNERSHIP

Process control is the key to the quality of our products and service. The enhancing of our processes in alignment with both experience and technological improvements will ensure a continuing marketplace for our products and service offerings. However, such changes must be controlled and never compromise the company's Quality objectives. Until such changes are proved and fully incorporated, then existing Procedures and Work Instructions will be followed.

All processes in New Era plc affecting quality are described in detail by either formal Procedures or Work Instructions. The Process described by a Procedure or Work Instruction is owned by the manager issuing it.

PROCESS CONTROL ACROSS
DEPARTMENTAL BOUNDARIES

New Era plc will, wherever possible, operate by Process Management. This frequently occurs by default, where the total process falls within the responsibility of one department.

However, there will be certain processes which span departmental boundaries and therefore involve Procedures and Work Instructions issued by different owners. In such cases the Quality Manager will assign an overall Process Manager who, in the opinion of the Quality Manager, has the major part of the process already within the scope of his or her management control. Any conflict of interests unable to be resolved locally will be brought to the attention of the "Quality System Review" for arbitration.

USE OF CONCESSIONS

Deviations from any formally documented process, described in the form of a Procedure or Work Instruction, is only permitted by the issuing of a Concession granted jointly by both the owning manager and the Quality Department.

RECEIVED MATERIALS AND SUB-ASSEMBLIES

Incoming materials and sub-assemblies destined for New Era plc products are required to be verified, tested or inspected in accordance with specifications as described in appropriate Work Instructions.

If incoming material is required urgently, then special concessionary authority can be obtained in liaison with the Production and Quality departments for its provisional release. In such circumstances all such material and sub-assemblies must be clearly marked or otherwise identified and records kept. Any such items are to be recalled or replaced in the event of them being subsequently found not to meet specified requirements.

PRODUCTION AND FINAL PRODUCT TESTING

Manufacturing procedures are available to describe the various "in-production" testing and verification which engineers must comply with on assembly lines. The Manufacturing Procedures may refer the engineer to other more detailed and specific Work Instructions, depending on the complexity of the tests.

FINAL PRODUCT TESTING

All completed products will undergo a three-part evaluation prior to being despatched to a customer. These are:

"A" Test   Basic workmanship standard.

"B" Test   Product SAFETY.

"C" Test   Functional.

PRESERVATION OF RECORDS

The results of all Production and Final Testing constitute Quality Records and must therefore be preserved, as described in Section 4.16 of this manual.

All inspection and test equipment used by Engineering and Production Departments will be formally controlled, maintained and calibrated where applicable to the manufacturer's specification.

The Production Department will maintain a register of all inspection and test equipment, including gauges and jigs in use throughout the company. This register will indicate the form and frequency of verification. The recall of equipment for calibration verification will be made from this register.

CALIBRATION

Calibration of indicating devices and measuring equipment will be traceable to National Standards. Records of calibration verification are to be held for a period of 3 years.

If equipment is found at any stage to be outside its calibration parameters then appropriate retrospective action will be put in place to evaluate and rectify any consequential adverse effects. Quality Procedures give precise instructions in this matter.

All departments holding test equipment are required to record their issue to staff and return the device promptly for re-evaluation when requested. All such equipment is required to clearly display a valid calibration label and a tamper-proof integrity seal.

Production procedures which specify the use of specific test or indicating equipment must not be deviated from or substituted other than by a formal Concession granted by the Design and Development Department.

All Test and Measuring equipment will, when not in use, be stored in a manner which preserves its integrity.

OVERVIEW

All assemblies and sub-assemblies which constitute sections of a New Era plc product will, throughout the production, carry a *Test Status Sheet*. This record will confirm, by a signature at each stage, that all relevant tests and test specifications required during the various production stages have been satisfactorily completed.

DEFINING OF TESTS

The details of the tests themselves will have been defined and issued by the Development Department and are to be found, as Work Instructions, in the addendum of the Design and Development Procedures Manual.

MAJOR UNITS

Those assemblies and sub-assemblies which have been defined as 'Major Units' by the Development Department are to be subjected to a final review by a representative of the Quality Assurance Deparment. The purpose of this review is to establish that the total testing programme has been satisfactorily carried out and that the "Test Status Sheet" is a true reflection of the final test status.

SEGREGATION OF NONCONFORMING MATERIALS

Materials and Products which fail to conform either to the purchasing or production standards of New Era plc are to be totally segregated. All such items are to be clearly identified by suitable labelling. The labelling should identify the nature of the nonconformity and the person who classified it unfit for use.

RECORDS

Records are to be maintained as to the disposal or reworking of nonconforming items. All departments where nonconforming material can be discovered, such as the Warehouse, assembly lines and Test Workshops, must have clearly identified areas reserved exclusively for the holding of nonconforming items.

Records are to be kept such that the statistical performance of subcontractors and suppliers can be measured in terms of nonconforming items. Appropriate action is to be taken to eliminate or reduce the supply of nonconforming items to New Era plc.

LOCAL REWORK

The Production Manager has the authority to carry out local reworking of nonconforming items if he considers it to be economically viable. In such cases the nonconforming item will still be registered as faulty against the supplier and entered into the appropriate statistics.

The same level of acceptance testing will apply following such a repair, as if the item were being received directly from the supplier.

CONCESSION

It is recognised that there may be isolated cases where for some reason a nonconforming part or sub-assembly may be left in a product during construction. The authority to take this action can only be granted by the Production Managers. The company Concession Procedure will be used to monitor this activity. In such cases the inclusion of the faulty item must be very clearly identified and recorded on the product's *Test Status Sheet*. The nonconforming item must be replaced before the completed product goes into Final Test.

SCRAP

The Production Manager has the authority to declare material as scrap and arrange for its disposal should he consider that its repair or rejuvenation is uneconomical.

The Corrective Action procedure in New Era plc is a uniformly managed process by which problems can be investigated and remedied. Its application is equally applicable to all departments in the company. It is also to be employed to resolve problems other than those directly related to production for example, administration or building services are equally applicable.

The Quality Manager is the owner of the Corrective Action Process which is fully described in the Quality Procedures.

The main purpose of the Corrective Action Process is permanently to eliminate current and potential problems in any part of the New Era plc organisation. Any employee can initiate a Corrective Action by sending a description of the problem to the Quality Department. A special form has been made available for this purpose.

The investigation of the subject problem will be managed and monitored by the Quality Department. The subsequent Corrective Action will likewise be tracked and evaluated by them. The originator of the Corrective Action request will be kept informed of the progress.

IMPORTANT NOTE

The Corrective Action procedure should not be confused with the New Era plc Suggestion Scheme.

The *Suggestion Scheme* is a communication platform by which employees can offer, for management's consideration, NEW and innovative ideas.

The *Corrective Action Procedure* is to find permanent solutions in situations where the agreed, documented processes appear to be failing, or no longer reflect current working practices.

Documented procedures are available in all departments of New Era plc which describe the handling, storage, packaging and delivery of all materials and finished products. These procedures must not be knowingly compromised.

The greatest care is to be exercised at all stages of production so as to minimise and/or eliminate damage. Particular vigilance needs to be applied to materials and components which are susceptible to discreet damage from such effects as electrostatic discharge, erosion, corrosion, chemical leakage and electromagnetic fields.

LIFE SPAN

Items held in storage are to be subjected to period inspection for their continuing suitability. All components with a declared life span are to be readily identified by suitable labelling. Attention should also be given to the stacking to ensure that a "first in, first out" practice is maintained and that physical crushing doesn't occur.

ELECTROSTATIC DISCHARGE PROTECTION (EDP)

All areas of the company where electronic components can be exposed are to be supplied with Electrostatic Discharge Protection facilities and all staff handling such components are to be instructed in their proper use. EDP facilities are to be functionally tested at meaningful intervals.

STOCKING LEVELS

Inventory levels in all stocking areas are to be maintained in accordance with the parameters set by Materials Planning Department. Annual stocktaking of all held materials and finished products is the responsibility of Purchasing Department. Cyclic stock-checking is carried out by a weekly rota and is the responsibility of the Warehouse Manager.

CUSTOMER-OWNED MATERIAL

Customer-owned material is to be appropriately labelled and fully segregated. In all other respects to is to be afforded the same conditions of care as is the stock owned by New Era plc.(refer to Section 4.7).

CUSTOMER SITE

The established practices of care and good housekeeping for materials and equipment are to be maintained on customer premises throughout the installation and servicing of any New Era plc products.

Quality records are those which can demonstrate the achievement of the New Era plc Quality System. The following list shows which are classified as Quality Records for the purpose of retention, archiving and disposal. Records are to be held by the owning department shown in the listing below.

Please note, the retention period is 1 full calender year from the completion of the activity.

Records to be retained	Held for one year by
Internal Quality Audits	Quality Dept.
Corrective Actions	Quality Dept.
Concessions	Quality Dept.
Customer Complaints	Quality Dept.
Test Status Sheets	Production Dept.
Subcontractor performance records	Production Dept.
Proof of calibration *(see Note 1)*	Engineering Dept.
Completed contracts	Marketing Dept.
EDP checks on workstations	Production Dept.
Quality of Work	All departments.
Stocktaking	Logistics Dept.
Mechanical drawings	Production Dept.
Circuit diagrams	Production Dept.
Documentation changes	Quality Dept.
Statistical performance	Quality Dept.
Back-up levels of software	All departments.
Subcontractor audits	Engineering Dept.
BSI Surveillance reports	Quality Dept.
Quality System Review records	General Manager

All the above Quality Records are to be archived for a further 12 months with the Quality Department. On or after their second anniversary they are to be disposed of.

Note 1   Calibration records (including certificates) must be retained for a total of 3 years.

Internal Quality Auditing is a continuous process by which New Era plc ensures that all departments of the company conform to the Quality System. It is a comprehensive scheme by which every element of the company's product manufacturing and installing activity is reappraised at least annually for compliance with documented procedures.

FREQUENCY OF AUDITS

The Quality Manager may increase the number of Internal Quality Audits beyond the minimum of one a year in any specific area of the company if he considers either:

- The department is too large a function to cover by a single audit.
- The department's activity is particularly significant in terms of deliverable quality to our customers.
- The department has undergone a change of manager or change in terms of responsibility.
- The department has been seen to be noticeably below the required standard.

DISCREPANCIES

Required Corrective Action arising from Internal Quality Audit, in the form of a discrepancy, is the responsibility of the respective line manager and must be cleared in an agreed reasonable time-scale.

REVIEWS AND REPORTS

The Quality Manager will provide and distribute a monthly summary report for all managers showing the trends being found in the current annual programme of Internal Quality Audits.

A formal detailed report on the Internal Quality Audit programme will be presented at the Quality System Review every 6 months.

TRAINING

It is recognised that one of the cornerstones of the company's Quality System is the Quality of the training invested in its people.

Certain training is mandatory for all employees and, wherever practical, should be carried out prior to any work responsibility being assigned. The following must be completed within 1 month of joining the company:

- Company Introduction Package.
- Health and Safety at work.
- The New Era plc Quality System.
- Electrostatic protection (for all Engineering staff).

It is the policy of this company that all employees shall be suitably trained to carry out the functions which they are assigned to perform. It is the responsibility of all managers with staff reporting to them to maintain a record of training undertaken. All employees will also have an agreed training plan to cover their development.

Wherever possible training, both technical and non-technical, will be formal and conducted by the Training Department. Use may also be made of external courses but enrolment on to such courses will be under control of the Training Department. There may be occasions when formal training is impractical. In such cases the manager must define the desired syllabus and organise local training or work experience. Such training must be recorded in the employee's training record.

Specialised departmental training will be arranged by each Department. Managers with staff reporting to them must review annually the training required for each post within their department.

SERVICING

The total responsibility for Customer Service is invested in those departments reporting to the Engineering Director. Engineering Division has total responsibility for all matters related to the preannouncement product evaluation, Installation and Servicing of the company products.

It is the policy of New Era plc to provide the highest quality of Customer Service available in the industry. The attainment will be constantly monitored against customer perception in the form of:

- Customer Satisfaction Survey.
- Customer Complaints.
- Response statistics.
- Customer equipment down-time records.
- Spare parts availability.

The above five key measurements will form part of the half-yearly Quality System Review.

A monthly Engineering Performance Report will be produced by Engineering Administration showing the current month's performance against agreed targets and the trend over the previous 11 months. The report will contain a narrative to amplify any adverse trend with a improvement plan. The Engineering Performance Report will be issued to the Managing Director and all departmental heads within the company.

STATISTICAL TECHNIQUES

Statistical analysis will be employed by all departments to track and demonstrate their performance against department and company objectives. The key areas to be monitored are shown below and demonstrate the company's commitment to Quality and Customer Care. There will be standard measurements and criteria across all departments where such activity is applicable:

- Customer Complaints
- Customer Satisfaction Surveys
- Quality Audits
- Quality of Customer Service in terms of:
  Time to answer incoming telephone calls
  Response time to service requests
  Down-time of Customer equipment
- Corrective Action
- Installed on time
- Spare parts availability

Monthly and year-to-date performance will be gathered and correlated by the Quality Department for distribution monthly to all departments. The Quality Department will also produce a 6-monthly statistical package for presentation at the Quality System Review.

Other statistics may be generated by individual departments to track the various parameters of the services they provide.

Part 3

Sample material

Forms, Procedures, Work Instructions, Job Description

CONTENTS OF PART 3

SET OF STANDARD FORMS

SAMPLE PROCEDURES, WORK INSTRUCTIONS, JOB DESCRIPTION.

Note:

You will see that in the "headers" of both the sample forms and the examples of documentation provided; I have followed the code:

> Round corners = Company-wide

> Square corners = Local use

Calibration History

Type	Make	Serial No	Bought	ID	

Date	Cert No	Period	Next	Held by	Dept	Notes

Antistatic Facility Tests

Form E1501
Issue 1

Please refer to documented procedures for details relating to the use and testing of antistatic facilities.

Month	Year

Owner/Bench	Date	Strap	Cords	Mat	Earth	Checked by	Comments

Service Request Record

Form E1901
Issue 1.

DATE	TIME	TAKEN BY	JOB NUMBER	
CUSTOMER		CONTACT	⁄TELE No	
ADDRESS			CUST No	

DETAIL OF PROBLEM

FAULT ISSUED TO	DATE ISSUED	TIME ISSUED	ETA TO SITE
	DATE ON SITE		REAL TIME TO SITE
CUST REF No	DATE CLEARED		CLEARED TIME

ADDITIONAL INFORMATION

ENTERED INTO DATABASE BY:

Customer Service Call Record

E 1902
Issue 3

CUSTOMER					CUSTOMER No		JOB No
	Date		Time		ENGINEER		
FAULT REPORTED					CONTACT		
ARRIVED							
COMPLETED					COVERED BY CONTRACT	Yes	No

REPORTED PROBLEM

REPAIR ACTION

PARTS USED   (Please note this is not an invoice)

Part No	Description	Qty.	Item cost	TOTAL

EQUIPMENT RETURNED TO CUSTOMER FULLY REPAIRED

TIME	DATE	CUSTOMER SIGNATURE	NAME

Dear Customer, if you could spare a moment we would be most grateful for your impression of our service - Thank you.	Very good				Poor
	1	2	3	4	5
How would you rate the manner in which New Era staff dealt with your telephone call to the Service Centre?					
How well did our engineer meet the agreed appointment time?					
How would you rate the professionalism of the visiting engineer?					
What impression did you get from the returned equipment - clean and demonstrated as working correctly?					
Finally, how would you rate the total service?					

190

QUALITY PROCEDURES

Issue Control Matrix

Form Q0501
Issue 1

Date of this issue   /   /

e = empty from this page   ◯ = changed this update

PROCEDURE	Page													
	1	2	3	4	5	6	7	8	9	10	11	12	13	14
1														
2														
3														
4														
5														
6														
7														
8														
9														
10														
11														
12														
13														
14														
15														
16														
17														
18														

Document Change Request

Form Q0502
Issue 1

DOCUMENT IDENTIFICATION

Document Change No
Issued by Quality Dept

TITLE	
SECTION	
ISSUE	
PAGE or APPENDIX	
REFERENCE	

Requested change

Example attached Y / N

Requested by _____ Print _____ Date _____

Department _____ Tele Ext _____

Owner's agreement   Signature _____

Print _____ Date _____

Owner's comments

Reissued by Q/Dept	Date	Issue No	Sign off

Customer Complaint Register

Form Q1401

Issue 1

No.	Date opened	Customer	Problem	Owner	Date Closed

Customer Complaint Record

Form Q1402
Issue 1

Customer _____   Complaint No [   ]

Customer contact _____   By letter/phone (delete)

Tele _____

Problem owner [   ]

DETAIL OF THE COMPLAINT

ACTIVITY DETAIL

Date	

Use reverse side to extend narrative

ATTACHMENTS

	Date
Received	
Acknowledged	
Target	
Closing letter	

SIGN OFFS

Owner	Print	
Quality Dept	Print	

Corrective Action

Form Q1403
Issue 1

Always send the original form to Quality Department when you have completed your Part.
Refer to Procedures for details.

C.A. Number (given by Q Dept)	

PART A - Originator to complete.

Request by	Dept	Phone	Date

Description of problem

You may offer a solution if you wish. Use the reverse of form if you need | Attachments y/n

PART B - Quality Department to complete.

Problem owner .... Department...............................

Response required from problem owner by ..../......./..........

Quality Dept contact is .... Date ..../......./......

PART C - Problem Owner to complete Parts C and D.

Response statement dated ..... /...../......

Target date for completion of Corrective Action ...... /...../......

PART D

Notification by owner of completion.

The Corrective Action as described in Part C of this report has now been implemented.

Signed .... Name ....

Date ..../......./......... Department ....

Corrective Action Register

Form Q1404
Issue 1

CA	DATES					
	Raised	Sent to Owner	Response req by	Response received	Target	CLEARED

Concession

Form Q1405
Issue 1

Concession No (issued by Quality Dept) [   ]

PART A   DESCRIPTION OF REQUIRED CONCESSION

Reference to documented procedure:
Use reverse of form also if required

Requested by	Dept	Tele extn	Date

PART B   PROCESS OWNER RESPONSE

Owner of process	Department
Comments	

Concession refused/granted until ...../......./.....

Signed off..........................
Print................................

PART C   QUALITY DEPT CONTROL

Reviewed by	Date	Reviewed by	Date
Reviewed by	Date	Closed by	Date

Quality audit record

Form Q1701

Issue 1

Audit of	By		Date	Audit No	

Area viewed	Pass Fail	Observations	Dis' #

DISCREPANCY & CORRECTION SUMMARY

Dis' #	Detail	Corrective action

Re-audit recommeded y /n   See Audit ID   for outcome

Auditor	Target date	Date cleared	Page ....
Auditee	Agreed	Accepted	of ....

Discrepancy report

Form Q1702
Issue 1

| Audit No | |
| Discrepancy No | |

Description of discrepancy

Auditor	Target clear date
Auditee	Date of audit

Corrective action taken

Auditee

| Accepted as cleared by Quality Dept | Page .... |
| Signed off   Date | of .... |

Test Status Sheet	Product type	Form P0001
	Serial No	Issue 2

Customer

Refer to WI No	Planned delivery date

Test	Checked by	Date	Comments	Fail Pass
1				
2				
3				
4				
5				
6				
7				
8				
9				
10				

Final product tests

	Comments	Sign off	Print name
A			
B			
C			

Quality control

Signed as of acceptable Quality.................................Print................... Date ....

PURPOSE

The purpose of this procedure it to provide a regulated process by which all documentation which is part of the Quality System, can be maintained at its optimum usefulness. This Document Change Procedure applies to any *registered* part of the documentation supporting the New Era plc Quality System. It can be initiated by either:

1.   A registered user of the document.
2.   The owner of the registered document.
3.   The Quality Department.

From whatever source the request originates, the form Q0502 is to be used as a control and record of authority for the change. The Quality Department will subsequently retain all completed forms Q0502 for a period of 1 year.

In all instances of changes to the documentation, the authority for the change must be granted by the Owner of the documentation. The management of the changes and the reissue of documentation to the registered users remains the responsibility of the Quality Department.

At the time of distributing updates of documents to the users, the Quality Department will always include a new "Issue Control Matrix" and an acknowledgement slip. Recipients of updated material are to file it correctly in the appropriate manual. They should then sign the acknowledgement slip and return it to the Quality Department. If the acknowledgement slip has not been returned within 1 month a reminder is to be sent to the recipient's manager.

ANNUAL REVIEW OF DOCUMENTS

All registered documentation is to be totally reviewed by its Owner at least every 12 months. The Quality Department will use this same procedure to initiate and control these scheduled reviews. This annual review may be brought forward at the request of the Owner should he consider it desirable. The Quality Department are to retain for a minimum of 12 months a copy of the previous issue of any part of the Quality documentation.

The process to effect changes is shown in the flowchart on the next page.

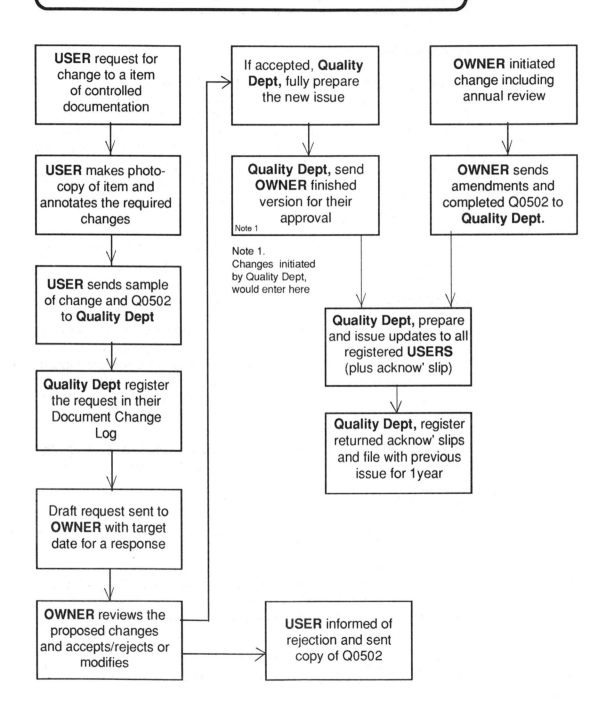

USER request for change to a item of controlled documentation

USER makes photo-copy of item and annotates the required changes

USER sends sample of change and Q0502 to **Quality Dept**

Quality Dept register the request in their Document Change Log

Draft request sent to **OWNER** with target date for a response

OWNER reviews the proposed changes and accepts/rejects or modifies

If accepted, **Quality Dept,** fully prepare the new issue

Quality Dept, send **OWNER** finished version for their approval
Note 1

Note 1.
Changes initiated by Quality Dept, would enter here

OWNER initiated change including annual review

OWNER sends amendments and completed Q0502 to **Quality Dept.**

Quality Dept, prepare and issue updates to all registered **USERS** (plus acknow' slip)

Quality Dept, register returned acknow' slips and file with previous issue for 1year

USER informed of rejection and sent copy of Q0502

Documentation Change Process

ANNUAL PROGRAMME

An annual programme of Quality Audits starting on January 1 are to be scheduled by the Quality Department to cover all the major departments of the company, including the Quality Department itself. This schedule must initially ensure that all working units headed by either a first or second line manager are subjected to a minimum of two Quality Audits per year. The Quality Manager may vary the frequency of Audits down to one per year if he is satisfied with the standard of previous inspections, or increase to maximum of four per year where, in his opinion, an excessive number of discrepancies were revealed in the past.

The planned dates of these scheduled audits are to be held *"confidential"* by the Quality Department until 5 working days prior to the audit.

RESOURCE

All first and second line managers are to make 3 days a year available to the Quality Manager to assist in the Quality Auditing of the company. Any manager assigned to the duty of Auditor has to have undergone training in the skills and procedures of such work prior to conducting any audit. The first audit carried out by a assisting manager will be observed by the Quality Manager.

Assisting managers, required to carry out audits on behalf of the Quality Department, will be given a minimum of 2 months notice.

PROCESS

The Quality Department will provide the auditor with a package consisting of:

- Q1701   Audit Record Form made out showing the department which is to be audited.
- QXXXX   An appropriate Check Sheet for the designated department.
- Q1700   BS5750 reference sheet.
- Q1702   Set of Discrepancy Detail forms.

The steps to follow are then:

1. The Auditor is to inform the subject department manager within 5 working days *(but no earlier)* of the scheduled audit date. The minimum notice is 48 hours.

2. Conduct the audit.

3. Complete all necessary paperwork while on-site and obtain agreement on any target dates for resolutions. Obtain the required signatures to complete the forms. Leave a copy of both completed Q1701and all Q1702s with the auditee.

4. Return all other items to Quality Manager. The Quality Manager will monitor and manage any discrepancies through to a resolution.

REVIEWS

A monthly statistical analysis of the Quality Audit programme is to be provided for the Managing Director with a short narrative to explain any trends. The Quality Manager will present a half-yearly statement at the Senior Managers' Quality Review Meeting. This presentation will describe any key areas of improvement or concern, along with a statistical analysis of the Quality Audit programme indicating the trends over the previous 6 months.

QUALITY AUDIT CHECKLIST (engineer and site)

This listing should be used as an aide memoire. It is not essential that all areas are addressed neither is the list exhaustive. Auditor may also select to view other areas not shown in this listing.

DOCUMENTATION

Does the engineer know where a copy of the following can be seen?
  QUALITY MANUAL
  QUALITY PROCEDURES
  ENGINEERING PROCEDURES
Does the engineer have a current issue of:
  LOCAL PROCEDURES
  ENGINEER'S HANDBOOK

GENERAL

TRAINING RECORDS	Are office records correct?
PERFORMANCE STATISTICS	Is engineer aware of key statistics?
TECHNICAL SUPPORT	Does engineer know how to evoke?
QUALITY OF WORK CHECKS	Look for recent evidence.
CALIBRATION	What was issued? Check it.
ESP OBSERVATION	Check the kit. Purpose known?
ESP FACILITY CHECKS	Records available?

CUSTOMER SITE

SITE LOG	Site and customer details correct?
RECORDS OF REPAIRS	Clear and complete detail shown?
MAINTENANCE (ROUTINE)	Scheduled and evidence of execution.
DIAGNOSTICS	Available?
ON-SITE SPARES	Defined and available?
CONSUMABLES	Oil, cleaners, fuses, "limited life" items.
MANAGEMENT CHECKS	Evidence of management checks
MANUALS	Listed and available?
TOOLS AND TEST	Listed and available? Check calibration.
SEGREGATION	Nonconforming products segregated?
SAFETY	Procedures observed?

JOB TITLE   Customer Service Supervisor

REPORTING TO   Customer Services Manager

REPORTING STAFF   4 Customer Service Coordinators

KEY TASK RESPONSIBILITIES

- The general daily supervision of the Customer Service Facility

- Produce a weekly staffing rota to ensure adequate staffing throughout normal business hours.

- Escalate to the appropriate Field Engineering Manager any Service Request which is in jeopardy of exceeding the agreed response time.

- Produce a daily back-up of the Customer Service database at the close of business each day (refer to Work Instruction E3001).

- Ensure that POWER DOWN procedures are well understood by the staff and conduct at least one unannounced "live" test a year.

- Gather new and updated information on engineers, customers and equipment. Input the database once a week with any new and confirmed information.

- Monitor "Time to answer the telephone" by the coordinators and produce weekly statistics of your findings for management.

- Conduct monthly Quality of Work checks on each member of your staff.

ADDITIONAL ASSIGNED SPECIAL DUTIES

- Prepare and run two "Customer Days" a year to illustrate to our customers the working of the Customer Service Facility.
  The invited group of customers per visit must not exceed 12 (target date for first session 1/11/92).

- Develop a method to ascertain the level of Customer Satisfaction with the service the department provides (target date 1/1/92).

PERFORMANCE MEASUREMENTS

- "Time to Answer the telephone" should not exceed 25 seconds.

TRAINING FOR ROLE

• Dealing with customers	2-day course (booked for Nov 91)
• Supervisor skills	3-day course (completed)

Signed as agreed.................   Line Manager...............

Date.............   Date ....

Peter Atkinson   Janet Frazer
Customer Services Supervisor   Customer Services Manager

ENGINEERING CUSTOMER DATABASE BACK-UP

The database holding all our current customer information, such as their addresses, the equipment they have installed, and any outstanding maintenance service they require, is held on a 60-million character storage device (hard-disk) in the IBM Personal Computer. This database also holds vital additional information regarding the engineers and the scope of their training. If, due to a malfunction, this information were lost or corrupted it would seriously impact the service to the customers. For this reason it is imperative that we make daily "copies" of the data so we could recover the situation. This process is known as *Back-up*. The Back-up process is to be carried out by the Supervisor at the end of each working day.

PROCESS

1. At the end of each working day take, from the Fire Safe in the manager's office, the set of disks marked with the current day (e.g. Friday).

2. Place the first disk of the set into the "A" drive and close down the flap.

3. Ensure that the PC screen is displaying the correct date and time. If incorrect then adjust.

4. From the Master Menu screen, select the option BACK-UP.

5. Follow the instructions displayed on the screen.

6. At the end of the process the screen will again display the Master Menu. At this stage remove the final disk from the "A" drive and return the full set of disks to the Fire Safe.

7. Enter details of your actions in the Daily Duty Log,
   e.g. BACK-UP TAKEN 19:37 hrs 30/8/91 (Friday) P.K.Thompson

Note: If you encounter any difficulties in carrying out this Work Instruction then contact the Technical Support Team for assistance.

All finished "New Era" products are to be subjected to the following three tests/examinations prior to packing for shipment. A controlled Work Instruction giving full details of the required tests has been prepared for each product and this must be used as a guide while conducting the tests. Obtain a current issue of the appropriate Work Instruction for the product and the product's Test Status Sheet (form P0001).

Ensure that all the required production tests and inspections have been conducted and passed. These should already have be annotated on the Test Status Sheet. If satisfactory, then continue with the following three tests.

"A" TEST - BASIC WORKMANSHIP

A close examination of both the exterior and interior is to be carried out. All plugged (i.e. not hard-wired) elements are to be temporarily removed to facilitate the tests. These removed elements must also be inspected. This visual examination should consider the general quality of manufacture, while giving particular attention to the following:

- The mechanical structure and physical security of major components.
- The aesthetic appearance of the unit including the overall cleanliness.
- The firmness of all electromechanical connections.
- That all the items shown on the *Shipping List*, including documentation, are present.
- That the "Made by New Era plc UK" label has been placed in a prominent position on the rear panel.

Carefully replace all the un-plugged elements.

Put a TESTED label on the rear panel and, if satisfactory, annotate as having passed the "A" Test with your initials and date clearly in biro, and then complete the Test Status Sheet.

"B" TEST - SAFETY

Carry out the "B" Test as described in the appropriate Work Instruction for the product. Annotate as having passed the "B" TEST with your initials and date clearly in biro and complete the Test Status Sheet.

"C" TEST - FUNCTIONAL

Before starting any "C" Tests ensure that the "A" and "B" Tests have been completed satisfactorily. The degree of final functional testing which can be carried out during the "C" Test varies from product to product since many products are sub-units of larger systems. However, for every unit, sub-assembly, machine and system there is a Work Instruction available, describing the minimum series of functional tests which the equipment must pass before it can be considered acceptable. All the appropriate tests must be carried out. When you are satisfied that the unit has passed its functional tests, then annotate the TESTED sticker as it having passed the "C" Test with your initials and date in biro and complete the Test Status Sheet.

In case of any item failing any of these tests it should be placed in the Rework Area for attention. The Test Status Sheet should adequately describe the reason for failing the tests.

In the case of a satisfactory product, the four copies of the Test Status Sheet are to be distributed as follows:

White	Attach to the tested product.
Blue	Held by Testing Section.
Pink	Quality Department.
Yellow	Spare copy, can be retained by Testing Engineer.

Finally, place any assembly which has passed all three tests in the Collect Area of the Testing Department.